12.1.04

To Prof. Smith,
with many, many
thanks.
Jane

WHY THEY COULDN'T WAIT

A Critique of the Black–Jewish Conflict
over Community Control in Ocean Hill–Brownsville
(1967–1971)

Jane Anna Gordon

D0161051

RoutledgeFalmer
New York and London

Published in 2001 by
RoutledgeFalmer
29 West 35th Street
New York, NY 10001

Published in Great Britain by
RoutledgeFalmer
11 New Fetter Lane
London EC4P 4EE

RoutledgeFalmer is an imprint of Taylor & Francis Group.

Printed in the United States of America on acid-free paper
Design and typography: Jack Donner

10   9   8   7   6   5   4   3   2   1

Library of Congress Cataloging-in-Publication Data

Gordon, Jane Anna, 1976–
   Why they couldn't wait : a critique of the Black-Jewish conflict over
community control in Ocean Hill–Brownsville, 1967–1971 /
by Jane Anna Gordon.
        p.   cm.
   Includes bibliographical references and index.
   ISBN 0–415–92909–1– (hardcover: alk. paper)—
   ISBN 0–415–92910–5– (pbk.: alk. paper)
   1. Ocean Hill–Brownsville Demonstration School District (New York,
N.Y.) 2. Minorities—Education—New York (State)—New York—History—
20th century. 3. Civil rights—New York (State)—New York—History—
20th century. 4. New York (N.Y.)—Race relations. I. Title.

LC3733.N7 G67 2001
306.43'2'097471—dc21   00–067066

To my beloved Lewis
And to the little beloveds,
Mathieu, Jenny, and Sula—
each a serendipitous gift,
each a new beginning

Those who profess to favor freedom yet deprecate agitation, are men who want crops without plowing up the ground; they want rain without thunder and lightning. They want the ocean without the awful roar of its many waters. . . . Power concedes nothing without demand. It never did and it never will. Find out just what any people will quietly submit to and you have found out the exact measure of injustice and wrong which will be imposed upon them, and these will continue till they are resisted with either words or blow, or with both. The limits of tyrants are prescribed by the endurance of those whom they oppress.

—Frederick Douglass,
West India Emancipation Speech, August, 1857

Contents

Preface, with Acknowledgments   xi

Introduction   1
The Need for Public Education in a Democratic Society

   1. Who Should Run the Schools?   7
      Decentralization and Community Control

   2. Black Power   25
      Failures of Integration and the Mobilization
      of a Community

   3. White Power   65
      The Construction of Jews as the Voice of Reason

   **4. When Some Workers Don't Look
      Toward the Left**   93
      The Battle with the United Federation of Teachers

Conclusion   117
A Question of Whose Children Benefit from Whose Labor

Notes   127

Works Consulted   145

Index   153

Preface, with Acknowledgments

We live in a political moment in which young women are encouraged to appear in the world as if they were purely of their own making. Strength, it would seem, is to have accomplished things without any assistance at all from others. Although there are, unfortunately, women who have had to go through the world completely alone, they would surely be the last to romanticize their lot. These fictions of denial and misrepresentation are a disservice on multiple grounds: They diminish the significant love and energy of the families and communities that have supported women and obscure the instrumental role that human networks play in the cultivation of self-determining young people.

I must admit that one of the things that excited me most when I was formally told that this book would be published was the opportunity to thank, in print, the many people who have cared for me. Although it is incomplete, a list of their names follows.

First, I must thank Karita dos Santos, my editor at RoutledgeFalmer, who fought for the publication of this book and the opportunities for authors without Ph.D's to have their scholarly work appear in print. Thank you also to Seema Shah, Jeanne Shu, and Lai Moy who coordinated the logistics and conducted the alchemy that would transform this manuscript into a book.

Many thanks are also due to Professor Carl Kaestle of Brown University, who escorted me through the field of the history of American education and patiently helped me turn my stumbling steps into an unfolding road of my own making.

Thank you to the Royce Fellowship Committee and its director Kris Hermanns, whose funds and recognition made completing this project much easier than it would otherwise have been.

Thank you to Julius Lester for offering me three hours of his precious time. In so doing he not only brought to life the subject under study here in all of its painful and humorous glory, but he also forced me to consider thoroughly the significance of what it means to be accountable to a human being with whom one really disagrees.

Thank you to all of the clinical professors of the Undergraduate Teacher Education Program at Brown University, particularly Bil Johnson. I am eternally grateful for our extended conversations about vampires and other things tragic and strange, Bil, and for your absolutely unwavering friendship and support.

Thank you, Professor Wendell Dietrich, my mentor, teacher, and friend, who, in his understated way, directed me toward life as an adult intellectual.

To Tony Perlstein, Suzanne Clark, Sage Wilson, Sara Mersha, Margo Guernsey, Kenneth Knies, Chas Walker, Eric Tucker, and Irene Tung, who regularly confirm that a sustained and critical engagement with Marxism is not the work of idle fools.

Thank you to everyone at the Institute for Elementary and Secondary Education: Chris Amirault, Carol Healey, Karen Lehrach, Emily McMains, Judy Williamson, and Kate Wilson. Your flexibility allowed me the time to finish this project. The interest you took in my family, in me, and in my ideas made me *want* to. I have learned a great deal from all of you and cannot imagine what the last few years would have been like without your life-affirming humor, loving honesty, and taste for fun.

Thank you to Rabbi Arnold Jacob Wolf, my first great teacher, who made it abundantly clear that a real commitment to a viable future for Judaism would require courage, hard work, and thick skin.

Many thanks to Tony Bogues and Geri Augusto, who have engaged me as informal mentors since our first meeting. Your tireless insistence on the indispensable need to read and to write works in Africana political thought has played a pivotal role in any and all of the good academic and political decisions I have made in recent years.

Thank you Dina Solomon, who despite my irascibility, continues to choose me as family.

Thank you to Paget Henry (*or should I say Uncle Paget?*) for the warmth and intellectual generosity he has always shown this *yout'*. Thank you also for the impromptu interview that made many submerged undercurrents surface.

Thank you Pat, Jack, Lori and Jo Garel, Mark and Robert Evans for making me one of your own. I treasure the profound connection I share with you and your past through the life that is Sula's.

Thank you to Mom, Dad, and Josh for bringing me into such a wonderfully rich and loving family full of magical and haunting temporal and spatial displacements. We have always lived in worlds that are at once the past, present, and future, the here and the there.

Thank you, Mathieu, for your patience as I worked to finish writing this book and for the pride you took in my doing it. The seriousness with which you took this project meant far more than you realized. Jenny, it is beautiful to watch you discover the value in writing and the magic in ideas. I was overcome by your candid love as you sat next to me, on that towering pile of books and papers, writing as I wrote the final sections of this book. Thank you to Sula, who communicates so much without prefabricated words. I so eagerly awaited your arrival, baby girl, and now cannot imagine what meaningful life was like before it.

To Lewis, with whom every day is too short. In the words of the great Abbey Lincoln, "Happiness, my love, is you."

Jane Anna Gordon
Providence, Rhode Island

Introduction

The Need for Public Education in a Democratic Society

I wrote this book because it needed to be written. I had read articles that were written in either the late 1960s or soon thereafter about different stages and layers of the conflict affecting the Ocean Hill–Brownsville school district and the many mentions made of it in the service of more extensive arguments concerning education and race relations in New York City. Although these articles varied considerably in tone, content, and their versions of "the facts," most of them shared a reluctance to frame the predominantly black and Puerto Rican community as sensible, or worse, reasonable.[1] The community in fact insisted that failing schools be reshaped immediately through practices informed by theories of committed Third World revolutionaries and by residents who had successful histories of working in public education. The Ocean Hill–Brownsville community was, however, for the most part, represented as an antidemocratic group of guerilla-like, aggressive, impatient, and power-hungry blacks. As a result, sophisticated articulations of the relationship between school reform and racial, social, and economic justice were left unheeded.

This story offers many significant lessons for contemporary activists. I was concerned that such lessons would be lost to racist imaginings posed as historical documentation. Unfortunately our society and its prevailing and structuring myths too often render such accounts believable to most readers. Such acts of erasure obscure insights that would otherwise benefit older and young generations seeking alternative senses of self-definition and can create a sense of hopeless nihilism in potential young activist-intellectuals. The story's ongoing relevance seems clear. Contemporary discussions surrounding public education have, for the most part, abandoned the language of "control" and "power." This is a fatal mistake.

No disenfranchised community has successfully changed the plight of its children without utilizing its public schools. Public education in the United States is designed, at least in theory, to foster economic and political independence in young adults who cannot afford to be educated through private means. Although some exceptional people clearly have, since 1945 it has been practically impossible to support a family or to go on to college and institutions of higher education without a high school diploma.

The diploma serves as proof both that one has done one's time and that one was able to survive, or even thrive, in these quintessentially U.S. institutions. This, in turn, is taken as evidence of one's possession of a particular brand of "cultural literacy," or a familiarity with certain sacred truths and myths, behavioral norms, and national aspirations. What is less often mentioned in a systematic manner is the ways in which the development of such knowledge is embedded in a larger, assimilative process. Although public schools have been sites of political contestation and negotiation, changing and being changed by successive generations of urban poor and immigrant children, this process short-circuited with the change in demographics that made blacks, Native Americans, and dark-skinned Latinos the majority in most urban public school classrooms. What became clear was that many of the employees running and manning the schools did not see these students as "their children." The failures or successes of these children would ultimately be extraneous to these teachers and administrators' estimation of the future.

The community under study here, and many other communities of color in the late 1960s, argued that their children had not been and would never be successfully educated or able to gain access to those opportunities made available through successful participation in public education, so long as such an attitude toward their children prevailed. They argued that they could and would care for their children as one does one's future and in so doing create the political infrastructure and sensibilities that they hoped would usher in a new social condition.

The years in which the events under analysis here took place, 1967 through 1969, were tumultuous years in U.S. history, marked especially, but not only, by struggles over race, education, and power. Civil rights demonstrations gave way to increasingly violent white backlash and rioting. While Martin Luther King Jr. broadened his tactics to focus on protesting the Vietnam War and to supporting striking sanitation workers, H. Rap Brown assumed leadership of the Student Nonviolent Coordinating Committee (SNCC) affirming the need for black organizations to be run by black people. Huey P. Newton's conviction for shooting a white police officer brought belated media attention to the work of the Black Panther Party.

The assassinations of King and Malcolm X left many black and white activists struggling for racial justice looking for direction. One focal point that most could agree upon was the need for an increasingly sophisticated treatment of these issues in institutions of education. In 1969, armed students at Cornell University demanded that the administration respond proactively to racial attacks on campus. Harvard University established an Afro-American Studies program, aiding the political work of students and faculty at other colleges and universities advocating for such measures.[2]

In the midst of all of this, several New York City leaders were attempting to decentralize the biggest school system in the United States. This move, arguably, facilitated a growing movement of poor white, Puerto Rican, and black communities efforts to control their local schools while failing to develop the structures essential for their success. One such effort took place in the community that is the subject of this study.

In Ocean Hill–Brownsville in 1967, two unlikely groups joined together to propose a scheme for greater community participation in the soon-to-be-opening local Intermediate School (I.S.) 55. The interest of the Ford Foundation and the New York City Board of Education and the emergence of one faction of leadership within the group led to the revision of the initial proposed program. Community participation was redefined: It did not only require parent-teacher committees and new programs, but dramatically increased localized control. An experimental district of eight schools was established. It was to be run by a locally elected governing board. The precise outline of this body's powers was never agreed upon. Although the local board effectively ran the schools for a two-year period, delineating their powers required a concerted decision for or against the possibility of poor communities having ownership, as they defined it, over local institutions. This decision was never formally made. Instead, a resolution was pushed by the New York City United Federation of Teachers (UFT), which, fearing the effects decentralization and community control would have on employees' job security, effectively demanded the dismantling of the experimental project.

The conflicts in Ocean Hill–Brownsville have been ingrained in American public memory as instances of black-Jewish antagonism, as the outgrowth of the struggle of the UFT to consolidate its power, and as the results of the beginnings of the decentralization of urban public schooling. My goal is neither to refute these readings nor to create a comprehensive account of the events. Rather, I wish to complicate these widespread characterizations of what transpired through analyzing why black and Puerto Rican efforts were perceived as they were and how these perceptions in turn created the conditions that ultimately led to the blocking of demands for community control.

In chapter 1, I attempt to distinguish between two educational movements—administrative decentralization and community control—through an interpretation of the work on public bureaucracies by the famed German sociologist Max Weber. In chapter 2, I explore the ways in which Black Power emerged as a theory of social action that mobilized black and other communities of color around school reform and transformation. In chapter 3, I look at the ways in which a particular commitment to liberalism on the part of many Jewish participants in the conflict led to a form of "White Power" ideology that rendered black efforts as intrinsically anti-Semitic and "illiberal." Finally, in chapter 4, I question why there was division rather than solidarity between the self-identified progressive UFT and the Ocean Hill–Brownsville community.

The events that took place in Ocean Hill–Brownsville thirty years ago still raise provocative and challenging questions: Who should control the education of disenfranchised youth and on what grounds? How do we evaluate the "success" or "failure" of innovative methods of school administration? Can liberalism adequately ameliorate racial injustice in the United States? What would a genuinely multiracial labor movement in the United States be like? Can there be a progressive political movement in the United States that does not take the mandates of racial and ethnic empowerment seriously?

To these questions, and many others, we now turn.

1

Who Should Run the Schools?

Decentralization and Community Control

Two competing reform movements structured debates around school management in the late 1960s. One was an impulse toward decentralization, and the other was toward community control. Many writers, then and now, confused or conflated these two currents, for both movements are informed by an effort to enlarge democratic participation in the running of public schools. They differ fundamentally, however, in the means and ends envisaged by their respective advocates. This difference, in turn, is rooted in fundamentally different understandings of the politics of schooling and its relationship to U.S. democratic life.

In what follows, I will argue that a call for decentralization—that is, the devolution of authority from the state to a more local public—set the stage for the effective mobilization of Ocean Hill–Brownsville, but that it was community control that the residents of that neighborhood and others like it clearly sought. To them, the structure of schools and schooling was less important than who was allowed to occupy positions of authority. They had found, repeatedly, that the attributes of the person filling the particular position had more to do with its definition than did any job description or credentialing requirements. I will conclude by laying out the analytical problem at the center of the conflict that transpired here: Why did the efforts of this black and Puerto Rican community, despite the way they were framed, demand a shift from decentralization to community control? Why was this distinction, negligible in discussions of the education of other communities, so central in this instance? Why were its attempts to partake in the running of its schools—attempts little different from those of other communities—seen to be irredeemably "political" in an educational system that sought to raise itself above the domain of politics?

Administrative Decentralization, A Definition

The term *administrative decentralization* refers to a way of structuring the public school system. It calls for duties and powers formally centralized at the Board of Education—the hiring and firing of teachers, principals, and other staff; the management of the budget; and the control over such things as curriculum design and supplementary programs—to be transferred to the level of the district, the borough, or the school.

According to Allan C. Ornstein, Daniel U. Levine, and Doxey A. Wilkerson, decentralization disperses the loci of authority. The nucleus of power remains with a central Board of Education, but the bureaucracy is broken into field or administrative units, themselves sometimes further divided.[1] By these means everyday control is, in principle, brought closer to the schools and community; also, closer communication exists between those schools and the center. This also induces a shift of influence from the latter to the field administration, where a number of services and departments are situated. Consequently, the field administrators and principals attain the power to make some decisions that were formerly made by the Board. "Accountability is still directed upward, not toward the community," write Ornstein et al., although field administrators are, ostensibly, sensitized to the needs and desires of neighborhood residents within their jurisdictions.[2] Because professionals and school board members retain authority under these arrangements, most educational functionaries find them highly congenial. At the same time, while this form of decentralization does not lead inevitably to increased community participation, it often does through the formation of advisory committees beyond the more traditional parent-teacher associations and other voluntary groups. These committees are only advisory. They may, however, include parents, local residents without children attending the public schools, teachers, administrators, students, and leaders of local business, political, religious, and social agencies.[3] What is more, they may operate at various levels of the system—the local school, the field or unit, or the central office—making recommendations and serving as liaisons between those levels. According to Ornstein et al.'s account, "Community participation is usually accepted and supported by teachers, administrators, and school board members, as well as by many minority parents and community leaders; it is, however, rejected by some critics of the teachers and schools and some radical groups because it does not transfer authority and power to the community."[4] We will return to this last objection, for within it lies the nub of an alternative model, a different politics of education.

This model of decentralization, part prescriptive and part descriptive, specifies "who" does "what" in structural terms, and how administrators, parents, residents, and others fit into a formal division of labor. But, crucially, it lacks an explanatory sociology: *which* members—by class, race, gender, and so on— of any community aspire to what kinds of participation and *why*. This is because, in the final analysis, the model is informed by pragmatic managerial considerations: centralized

Boards of Education are far too removed from the districts under their control, and far too overloaded to respond effectively to grass-roots needs.

Two Views of Decentralization

In 1993, looking retrospectively at decentralization efforts over the previous thirty years, David Tyack argued that "When Americans grow dissatisfied with public schools, they tend to blame the way they are governed. There is too much democracy or too little, critics insist, too much centralization or too little, too many actors in policy formation or too few."[5] Although a profound distrust of government and centralized administrative bodies in general is a common feature in many U.S. citizens, they have, in the words of Tyack, "also asserted a utopian faith that, once the right pattern of school governance was found, education would thrive."[6] The structure of the public school system has long been both demonized and romanticized; it is, at once, a potential panacea and the nemesis of the prevailing social order.

Policy talk today about "restructuring," "choice," and "national standards," argues Tyack, citing the Reports of the U.S. Department of Education (1991) and the National Governors' Association (1991), is only a recent episode in a cyclical debate that is a century and a half old. Those advocating each new stage of centralization or decentralization have always promised significant change. The intensity of the claims made on behalf of each organizational structure were not qualified at all as popular opinion swung between them: whichever was accepted as the way of one period would be dangerous delusion in the next. Many Progressive era social critics, for example, joined business leaders in urging the centralized control of schools, emulating the consolidation of vast corporations early in the twentieth century. Today they urge "restructuring" or decentralization, again citing business practice (this time in a neoliberal key) as a model.

At the same time, Tyack further observed, for all the talk of theorists, policymakers, and activists, there are strong forces of continuity in the everyday lives of schools. This, as historians and organizational sociologists are coming increasingly to appreciate, derives from the force of common cultural beliefs—what Tyack calls the "invisible hand of ideology"—in shaping institutions. The allusion to Adam Smith is significant. It implies that attention to the formal powers of officials and to organizational structures, descriptive or prescriptive, tells only part of the story.[7] As J. G. March and J. P. Olsen point out, "Institutions are neither simply arenas for individuals to pursue their own agendas nor creatures of outside forces, ever permeable to the winds of change."[8] They sustain themselves over long periods of time, resisting or co-opting demands for change—precisely because their ideological *core* endures over the long run. "Even the Great Depression, a major economic catastrophe," writes Tyack, "had surprisingly little impact on public schools."[9] Perhaps this observation is less surprising than we might initially think, for, after all, it is during times of crisis that we most consistently look backward, to a past that seems as real as it is imagined, for strategies and theories that "have worked."

Let us now turn to a second scholar, to political scientist Richard Elmore. Elmore is equally concerned with the continuity and reform of schools. Addressing the apparent sharp divide between the promises of alternative structures and their effects, Elmore writes, "In any specific case, decentralizing reforms seem, at least on the surface, to provide very plausible answers to the ills of public education. In general, however, repeated cycles of centralizing and decentralizing reforms in education have had little discernible effect on the efficiency, accountability, or effectiveness of public schools."[10] These cycles, he goes on to argue, have their own logic. Thus an event, often somewhat unclearly, will trigger a call for the centralization or decentralization of educational administration. This is followed by a doctrinal debate about the relative merits of centralization and decentralization. "At any given point in the debate," he notes, "the 'correct' or 'enlightened' position is usually clear: it is the opposite of whatever was previously correct."[11] Elmore argues that each position has its accompanying cliches that can be recited when necessary by the advocates of the day. In the end, he asks, "What practical consequences follow from the centralization or decentralization of administrative or political responsibility in American education?"[12]

Elmore concludes that the cyclical nature of the thinking regarding these alternative policies reveals their ultimate superficiality: The importance of the process of debate seems to transcend concern over the significance of the measures themselves; the research informing those in heated battle is characterized by a "virtually complete disconnection" between structural reform and the content of the classroom itself.[13] This disjuncture allows for reforms that "wash over the educational system," consuming large amounts of resources— money, time, the energy of parents, teachers, and administrators, and the political capital of elected officials—with, at best, few results, and at worst, detrimental ones. "Because the process of centralization and decentralization is cyclical," says Elmore, and "because each cycle leaves behind some vestige of its reforms, the cumulative effect of several cycles of reform is to make the educational system more complex, less accessible to its clients, less comprehensible to those who work in it, and therefore less manageable, even though each reform, taken by itself, is predicated on the assumption that it alone will make the system simpler, more comprehensible, and more manageable."[14] Neither approach has enabled the school system to respond more effectively to what is needed and in the meantime, argues Elmore, the practical question of whether students' learning is improving is overlooked. This seems to be a serious overstatement. The works of Theodore R. Sizer and Anthony Bryke, for example, offer analyses of the differences that structural changes do and do not make.[15] Nevertheless, Elmore suggests that an explanation for this ongoing delusion, which is directly relevant to my argument here, requires us to take a step back and look at the ways in which school reformers envision the relationship between public schooling and democratic participation. He observes that questions about the merits of different forms of school structure have been overlaid onto a schizophrenic view of the relationship between democratic participation and institutionalization, and turns here to political scientist James Morone's description of the "democratic wish."[16]

"American political culture," writes Elmore, "is based on two fundamental convictions: faith in government, based on direct, communal democracy; and the fear that concentrations of power in governmental institutions are dangerous to individual liberty."[17] Because of these two beliefs, American political institutions are often designed to mediate conflicts that arise from democratic participation and, at the same time, are institutions with constraints against impositions on liberty. To limit the power of these institutions, responsibility over their management is often dispersed. The result, says Elmore, is institutions that are "vulnerable to stalemate," and that are especially good at "frustrating attempts" to change them.[18] Periodically, the response of reformers is "to act on the democratic wish to return power to 'the people,' through reforms that push decision-making out into smaller, simpler, more directly accountable institutions."[19] Elmore draws the parallel with decentralization efforts. These rarely displace existing institutions, however; for the latter are laced with the products of earlier attempts to disperse power. Even when new institutional forms do emerge, they quickly become routinized. Attention to their maintenance "displaces the fervor of the reforms that spawned them," provoking opposition and the mobilization of new groups seeking change.[20] This generation seeking another set of institutions—more responsive to "the people," as defined by this group of reformers—will soon face another, creating a climate of futility.[21]

Tyack and Elmore present a picture of the contradictions at the root of decentralization efforts. Although the particularities of their characterizations are somewhat different, each speaks to a fundamental misunderstanding of the workings of schools and their being embedded in larger historical processes. In Tyack, this is diagnosed as a lack of understanding of the role of ideology in efforts to dictate change; Elmore sees it as a misconception on the part of education policymakers, who turn to schools in their attempt to foster the growth of democratic institutions. Neither suggest that the limitations of these debates and their practical consequences may lie in their ultimate reformism, that there could be a substantive break from the cyclical nature of these changes if disenfranchised groups, representing and embodying "the underside of modernity," were given control to run their schools.[22] In this instance, people who understood the role ideology plays in sustaining political continuities, and who were very familiar with the contradictions of democratic life, could have envisioned alternatives to the futile efforts that preceded them. Or perhaps, these authors would argue, armed with administrative powers, this alternative leadership would, like the countless others before them, struggle as they tried to bring democratic life to bureaucratic institutions.

This pursuit of democracy in education is not confined to decentralization models, however. Let us now turn to an alternative, that articulated in the terms of *community control*. From there we will consider the distinct sociological positions occupied by advocates of decentralization and community control, respectively. This will prepare the ground for an analysis of the troubled case of Ocean Hill–Brownsville.

Community Control, A Definition

Although administrative decentralization and community control are assumed to be synonymous in common parlance, they are not, in fact, the same thing. Community control also refers to a model of educational governance; it presumes decentralization but does not merely move authority over schooling down a bureaucratic hierarchy. Instead, it calls for the transmission of that authority directly into the hands of specified individuals in the community. Urban blacks have often demanded this version of decentralization, not only in regard to schools but also with respect to other social institutions. That schooling has been unresponsive to the needs and interests of children of color is offered as justification. Demonstrating that "professionals" have failed to educate these children, white liberals, black militants, and a growing number of black moderates have argued—and continue to argue—that "the 'community' ought to be given a chance to succeed, or at least to fail, and on its own terms."[23] Such groups usually advocate the decentralization of schools within existing frameworks, but in a way that facilitates public control, or at least allows greater popular input.

An elected local school board functioning under specific guidelines and in conjunction with the Board of Education requires legal provision in order for it to achieve community control thus conceived. Substantively, this means that local and central school boards share decision-making authority and power. Carried out to its fullest extent, such mutuality implies total governance by the community over school personnel, including hiring, firing, and promoting; curriculum, course electives, the selection of textbooks, and evaluation; student policy, student-teacher relations, discipline, and testing; and financing, from the solicitation of federal funding to the determination of budgets. In this way, the authority over education professionals and state institutions is at once abridged and passed into collective hands. This kind of democratization is, according to Ornstein et al., "rejected by most teachers and administrators, especially [by] whites in big-city schools who fear reverse discrimination, [increased] quotas in hiring and promotion policies, and even loss of their jobs."[24] These teachers, many white, some black, often invoke "professional expertise" as playing an indispensable role in protecting what is democratic in these institutions.[25]

The arguments against community control are by now fairly standard: that expectations of it are subject to the same delusions used by Tyack and Elmore to describe the vehemence of arguments for and against decentralization; that it impedes integration and balkanizes cities; that parents and local residents (especially in low-income areas) lack the experience and ability to deal with complex educational issues; that community control undermines the merit system and weakens the teachers' union; that it distracts attention from the greater need for money to educate children; that it is likely to encourage reverse discrimination and lead to a rejection of white participation.[26]

These contentions have elicited responses from proponents of community control. On the one hand, they point out that by the late 1960s, schools in most cities were more segregated and are even more so now, than prior to the Supreme Court's famous *Brown* decision of 1954; they assert, too, that most whites and now many blacks do not want to "integrate," that, in any case, "integration" connotes white supremacy and black assimilation, and that most cities are already balkanized.[27] On the other hand, proponents argue that parents are motivated to action *because* their children are failing in inadequate schools and that high quality education is their objective.[28] As for inexperience, incoming local school board members can be trained. Regarding ineptness, how can we determine ability until these people have been allowed the opportunity to run their schools? Furthermore, they add, competitive examinations for educational professionals are "white-oriented"; there is insufficient evidence to prove that only those who pass the exams are "fit and qualified" to perform their jobs.[29] On the question of the teachers' union, protagonists of community control note that in most cities the union is already splintered by political and racial issues; it is weakened further, not by democratized education, but by depleted school budgets, by citizens' revolts against higher taxes, and by the prevailing surplus of teachers. In addition, citizens do not accept the fiscal thesis that states that more money *is* a requirement for reform because nothing suggests that it is either better raised or spent by centralized rather than local authorities.[30] Finally, what about four hundred years of white racism? Black children need an education that will help them deal with that legacy. White personnel sensitive to the needs and interests of African-American youth can and should be encouraged to remain in their schools; this does not suggest inevitable reverse racism.

Over time, the case for community control also expanded to include other claims: that by imbuing them with pedagogic authority, teachers and administrators would be made accountable to the people; that it would more likely lead to educational innovation and ensure greater parental and public participation; that it would enable local school boards to hire *more* qualified principals and superintendents—people who could relate to children from the inner cities and serve as emulative models; that it would enhance flexible hiring and promotion practices, and attract teachers and administrators with more initiative and innovative capacity; and, most important of all, that it would raise student achievement and promote self-government for blacks, as well as for other minorities.[31]

These more elaborate claims called forth yet further critical disagreements. How, it was asked, could anyone be so sure of the prospective performance of teachers and administrators appointed by "the community"—or, for that matter, of its representatives and parents—in running an effective school system? After all, experts in the field found it well-nigh impossible to do this.[32] On what grounds could it be concluded, as community activists appeared to have done, that black student failure was to be blamed on professional educators? What about the effects of variables such as the home, the neighborhood, and other social factors? Could local school boards not likely become mired in the politics of self-interest and ideology? Could the majority of people, including parents, not become indifferent to educational issues, not participate in school meetings, and fail to vote on relevant matters? As a result, it may well be assumed then that politically oriented groups, ranging from black militants to white segregationists, would gain control of the schools for their own purposes, just as they had in the past in New York City and Detroit. This, in turn, would surely lead to increased ethnic and racial favoritism in appointing and promoting administrators, replacing competitive performance, experience, and objective tests with patronage, nepotism, and pork-barrel practices. At the very least, it was argued, reformers should pilot test the assumption that student achievement would be raised before mass changes were implemented; and this all the more so, since no evidence indicated that black teachers and administrators would necessarily be more successful at raising achievement among black students. To this was added another point of criticism: that community control would surrender the suburbs to white domination, leaving blacks in control of inner-city neighborhoods with depleted finances and real problems of decay, drug addiction, violence, crime, traffic congestion, pollution, and overpopulation.[33] This, in turn, would thwart future possibilities for school desegregation, which should have been the immediate goal of educational reform.

Situating all this in the historical context of the present study, it is notable that, by the late 1960s, the moment with which we are concerned here, the argument for and against community control was articulated entirely in terms of black–white relations. Why? In order to answer this fundamental question, let us look first at the structural position of blacks under contemporary U.S. public bureaucracies.

American Public Bureaucracies—A Weberian Reading

Although the great German sociologist Max Weber expressed different analytical concerns from the authors considered above, he does offer us something useful in his attempt to systematize the relationship between democratization and bureaucratization in modern society.[34] Weber's analysis will not only help us with our own understanding of this relationship, but it will also be necessary in addressing some of the questions raised in the chapters that follow. Weber's writing on the "rationalization" of education suggests that the very structures required by Western democracy predetermine the form and the ultimate futility of the kind of debates we have just discussed.

For Weber, "The decisive reason for the advance of bureaucratic organization has always been its purely technical superiority over any other form of organization."[35] Bureaucratic organization may be compared to other systems of organization in the way that mechanical modes of production are comparable to nonmechanical equivalents. Primarily a product of the modern world, bureaucracy is clearly a feature of capitalist market economies, which require that the official business of administration be precise, ongoing, and rapid. Weber argues that above all, bureaucratization offers the optimum possibility for creating and executing specialized functions according to "purely" objective considerations. The "objective" discharge of business, he concludes, means operation according to discernable rules and "without regard for persons," in contrast to what he terms premodern, feudal forms.[36] Writes Weber:

> When fully developed, bureaucracy's . . . specific nature, which is welcomed by capitalism, develops the more perfectly the more the bureaucracy is "dehumanized," the more completely it succeeds in eliminating from official business love, hatred, and all purely personal, irrational, and emotional elements which escape calculation.[37]

Such depersonalization is indispensable to the smooth running of capitalist societies. For in the effort to treat people fairly and efficiently, we must create neutral subjects. In Weber's view, these impersonal forms flourish in democratizing countries, which attempt to set up legal guarantees that will ensure "equality before the law."[38] This requires an effort to maximize "objectivity," in contrast with the arbitrary, personal discretion entailed in the "grace" of old-style patrimonial domination; for it is only through rationalized measures that one can clearly distinguish an "objective" legal order from the individual "subjective rights" that it guarantees. Under such conditions, public law regulates the relations between public authorities and their dealings with their subjects; private law regulates the relationships among the governed themselves. This distinction, Weber argues, presupposes the conceptual separation of the "state" as an "abstract bearer of sovereign prerogatives" and generator of "legal norms," from all authorizations provided by persons as individuals.[39] The dichotomy of private and public first emerged in urban communities, where offices devolved by means of periodic elections rather than as a matter of personalized right.[40] Yet full and principled development of the separation of public and private would only take place once the administrative management was thoroughly depersonalized.[41]

Although the separation of public and private, the objective and the personal/partisan are taken in the West to be the *sine qua non* of democratic systems, it creates significant problems for those whose political aims are predicated on democratic participation. For these are idealized distinctions conceived and described in theory; in actual practice, in real historical contexts, how effectively can these separations be maintained? For as they develop, bureaucracies concentrate the material means of management in the hands of "masters" who are starkly distinguished from those they govern.[42]

Weber recognizes this as a substantive problem. He notes that among the mass of the governed, questions about authority or the power of legitimated bureaucratic officials tend to be understood as partisan issues, oriented toward some concrete instances and persons. This inevitably conflicts with the formalism and "objectivity" of bureaucratic ideals. Furthermore, those lacking material means will inevitably believe that justice and administrative authority should compensate for their economic and social plight. Yet such demands can only be pressed if couched in particular and partisan terms—the very "case to case" terms that, Weber tells us, is the "horror" of the bureaucratic reasoning and its principle of "equality before the law."[43] What this means is that the dream of eliminating such systems becomes ever more utopian; the material fate of the governed depends increasingly on the smooth running of the administrative system, and hence they are unable to remove or replace the bureaucratic apparatus once it is put in place. The whole edifice relies on trained experts, a functional division of labor, and an acceptance of the need for virtuoso-like mastery of distinct and carefully integrated functions. In this regard, bureaucratic administration of democratic institutions does not necessarily mean increased power and authority of the governed within the overall social structure.

Weber explicitly applies these systematic insights to the nature of "training and education," arguing that underlying many of the struggles in this domain, at least in the modern world, lies the "irresistible expanding bureaucratization of all public and private relations of authority and by the ever-increasing importance of expert and specialized knowledge."[44] Here as elsewhere, once it is fully established, bureaucracy is among those social structures that are the hardest to destroy, for it has become the very medium of acceptable struggle. Indeed bureaucracy is the legitimate means of making partisan "community action" into rationally ordered "societal action."[45] Little wonder, then, that community efforts to counter what are experienced as disadvantages in the face of bureaucratic power should so often be discounted as partisan politics, whether in respect of schooling or any other sphere of democratic entitlement.

Weber's analysis of bureaucracy has many implications; significant for our purpose is his insight concerning the ways in which bureaucracy effectively structures relationships of power, legitimating particular kinds of action and discrediting others. His model suggests that certain overarching processes intrinsic to modern democracies function in counter–democratic ways, presenting enduring paradoxes of enfranchisement and exclusion that determine not only the distribution of material means and "cultural capital," but the very means of acceptable struggle themselves. The people to whom we now turn are exactly those whom Weber suggests are structurally underserved by this version of democratic organization and its prevailing discourses.

The Struggle for Community Control in Ocean Hill–Brownsville

Simply stated, what the primarily black population of Ocean Hill–Brownsville demanded in the late 1960s was that the duties allocated to, and required of, decentralized boards be handed over to their community. They were less concerned with structural arrangements per se than with the personnel who occupied positions of power. Here lies a major distinction between decentralization and community control models: The former focuses primarily on specified structural arrangements, the latter on the identity of the people located in them. Although the structural question can be on the office of *who* makes decisions—principals, superintendents, teachers, a mixture of both, and so on—community control may be such that it sometimes does not challenge the *office* of who makes decisions but the *background* of who occupies the office; community control sometimes involves a demand for the officers to emerge *from the community*. Advocates of community control often welcome decentralization efforts because they seem to make it easier for communities to get involved and to claim positions of power. But the distinction between the two models is central to the conflicts that occurred in Ocean Hill–Brownsville. What began as a legislative move toward decentralization was taken by the community as an ideal time to try, once and for all, to gain control over their schools, just as suburban parents had done long ago, without struggle.[46] This required that the occupants of the newly decentralized positions of authority be designated an essentially political process. Some protagonists of decentralization saw this move for community control as a perversion of their principles. Others were simply embarrassed by it because the decentralization movement had always claimed to be apolitical, and this ostensible rush to politicize the control over schools appeared to violate that claim.[47] Note the double standard here: When a predominantly black community expressed the desire to govern its own schools in the same way as suburban whites did, its actions, particularly its efforts to redefine job prerequisites for its district, as had many before them, were criticized as "political"—which, as we will see, has been read as assertively nationalistic, self-interested, and antiliberal.

In Ocean Hill–Brownsville, the pursuit of educational autonomy was informed by the Civil Rights movement and the rise of Black Power. Of course, not everyone had participated in these movements, or followed their every detail. However, many of those in positions of leadership had participated in freedom rides and voter registration campaigns as members of activist groups, or knew people who had. Others had studied the writings and listened to the speeches of activist intellectuals like Malcolm X and Stokely Carmichael. While residents of the neighborhood were disenfranchised, desperately poor, and isolated, they were nonetheless driven to action by the mood of a particular historic moment whose currents were felt throughout black America.

2

Black Power

Failures of Integration and the Mobilization of a Community

Different scholars have mapped divergent intellectual genealogies for the Black Power movement. Speaking about Black Power as represented by Stokely Carmichael to an audience of London Marxists in 1967, the great Trinidadian revolutionary and political theorist C. L. R. James argued that the banner, Black Power, would become one of the greatest of that time. Although, he qualified, only time itself could tell. Black Power had emerged from a deep-rooted and well-conceived intellectual and political legacy—beginning with the egalitarian claims of the bourgeois revolution as formulated by Jean-Jacques Rousseau and Thomas Jefferson on the one hand and the critique of its contradictions by such diverse black intellectuals as Booker T. Washington, W. E. B. Du Bois, Marcus Garvey, Aimé Césaire, George Padmore, and Frantz Fanon on the other. This critical tradition would lead, he claimed, to the kind of activism that would eventually foster an international socialist movement. James sought to "get rid, once and for all, of a vast amount of confusion arising, copiously, both from the right and also from the left."[1]

James suggested that this need to trace the lineage emerged in response to the view of many in both England and the United States that Black Power and its advocates were "some sort of portent, a sudden apparition, some racist eruption from the depths of black oppression and black backwardness."[2] James argued, instead, that Black Power was actually a high point in thought on the "Negro question," which dated back more than half a century. He argued that this period of greatness grew under the leadership of young, worldly people, many well-traveled Caribbeans, living in the center of advanced U.S. society. They envisioned themselves as part of a larger Third World struggle for colored power. This multiracial platform was encompassed under the slogan of Black Power because it had been blacks as a group who had suffered most and longest under the weight of imperialism. "The kind of impact the Negroes are making," concluded James about this growing American movement, "[was] due to the fact that they constitute[d] a vanguard not only to the Third World, but constitute[d] also that section of the United States which [was] most politically advanced."[3] James was referring to northern urban centers of the United States, which he, incorrectly, compared favorably to rural Southern regions in which armed whites kept blacks from exercising their democratic rights to vote. James, I suppose, had not heard about efforts to integrate schools in Queens, New York, in this period, nor of the many white mobs in northern cities who descended upon and decimated black communities through fear of the expectations of returning black veterans after both world wars.

William L. Van Deburg agreed that Black Power represented a peak, though he contextualized it within the rich intellectual history of black nationalism. Along with the post–World War I organizational efforts of Marcus Garvey and the United Negro Improvement Agency (UNIA), Black Power emerged "whenever an unwilling exile began to (1) question and then reject their presumed status as 'inferior' vis-à-vis whites; (2) recognize the need for intraracial solidarity;

(3) proclaim their intellectual independence; (4) employ shared experiences with bondage, caste, and folk culture to shape countervisions of the racial future." Wrote Van Deburg, its essential spirit "was the product of generations of black people confronting powerlessness—and surviving."[4]

The battle cry of Black Power was most clearly heard in 1966, when Trinidadian-born Stokely Carmichael (Kwame Ture) and H. Rap Brown (Jamil Andullah Al-Amin), the leadership of the Student Nonviolent Coordinating Committee (SNCC), previously committed to interracial activism through activities like freedom rides and voting rights campaigns, decided that it was politically necessary to keep non-blacks from participating in the group's future work. At this point, white members were asked to leave the organization. Carmichael argued that black people needed to occupy positions of authority in organizations devoted to the cultivation of black communal life.

Van Deburg argues that Black Power activists made use of the resources of the radical black intellectual tradition, including the work of some nationalist thinkers. All saw black accommodationism in integration-oriented politics and suggested that separatism would enable the development of political, economic, psychological, and cultural dimensions of black life, which would encourage self-determination. Black unity would require individual and communal transformation. The end result would be black recognition of their common grievances.

In the late 1960s, the most widely read texts by urban communities of color were *The Autobiography of Malcolm X* and Stokely Carmichael and Charles Hamilton's *Black Power*. Both of these works advocated that black communities recognize and identify what might appear as a set of discrete forms of discrimination as part of a larger "white power structure." Wrote Carmichael and Hamilton:

The man in the ghetto sees his white landlord come only to collect exorbitant rents and fail to make necessary repairs, while both know that the white-dominated city building inspection department will wink at violations or impose only slight fines. The man in the ghetto sees the white policeman on the corner brutally manhandle a black drunkard in a doorway, and at the same time accept a pay-off from one of the agents of the white-controlled rackets. He sees the streets in the ghetto lined with uncollected garbage, and he knows that the powers which could send trucks in to collect that garbage are white. When they don't, he knows the reason: the low political esteem in which the black community is held. He looks at the absence of a meaningful curriculum in the ghetto schools—for example, the history books that woefully overlook the historical achievements of black people—and he knows that the school board is controlled by whites. He is not about to listen to intellectual discourses on the pluralistic and fragmented nature of political power. He is faced with a "white power structure" as monolithic as Europe's colonial offices have been to African and Asian colonies.[5]

In a footnote Carmichael and Hamilton added that although studies had shown that business and professional men made up only 15 percent of the population nationwide, they constituted 76 percent of school boards in a national sample.[6] To draw attention to the relationship between economic exploitation, disenfranchisement, and the failure of public education in communities of color, they added:

It is a stark reality that the black communities are becoming more and more economically depressed. Lest someone talk about educational preparation, let it be quickly added here that unemployment rates in 1965 were higher for non-white high school graduates than for white high school drop-outs. Perhaps the most striking feature . . . is the fact that a non-white man must have between one and three years of college before he can expect to earn as much as a white man with less than eight years of schooling, over the course of their respective working lives.[7]

Carmichael and Hamilton argued that the only adequate response would require black leadership and control and "emphasizing race in a positive way: not to subordinate or role over others but to overcome the effects of centuries in which race has been used to the detriment of the black man."[8] Community members in Ocean Hill–Brownsville were familiar with, and often sympathetic to, the logic of these arguments. Such contentions appeared then, as they do now, both well-informed and convincing.

Malcolm X had predicted that attempts on the part of black people to change their condition would be construed as violent. In concert with Frantz Fanon, who had insisted that decolonization, even before the emergence of armed struggle, is always experienced as violent, Malcolm X recounted that despite speaking repeatedly of a profound shift in the nature of his political thought on the question of armed struggle, white reporters always sought to connect him to the word *violence*. He reflected toward the end of his life:

> You watch. I will be labeled as, at best, an "irresponsible" black man. I have always felt about this accusation that the black "leader" whom white men consider to be "responsible" is invariably the black "leader" who never gets any results. . . . I have been more reassured each time the white man resisted me, or attacked me harder— because each time made me more certain that I was on the right track.[9]

Although prevailing ideologies made this work easy, J. Edgar Hoover, infamous head of the FBI, invested government time and resources in the project of painting Black Power activists as violent criminals. In his August 25, 1967, Memorandum to the Special Agent in Charge, Albany, New York, a meorandum devoted to the discussion of counterintelligence programs to protect the nation against the threat to internal security posed by "black nationalist–hate groups," Hoover encouraged agents to "endeavor to establish the unsavory backgrounds [of the black leadership]."[10] Government employees were to "be alert to determine evidence of misappropriation of funds or other types of personal misconduct on the part of militant nationalist leaders so any practical or warranted counterintelligence [could] be instituted."[11] In other words, rather than acting in accordance with the legal, political, and civil ideal of assuming innocence in the absence of convincing evidence to the contrary, a deliberate governmental decision was made to tailor public opinion and media representations in ways that forever link Black power and supporters to crime.

The political climate for urban communities of color was thus one of growing awareness of the structural dynamics behind the social, economic, and racial realities they were living and the claustrophobic surveillance of their efforts to transform those realities. Let us now turn to the Ocean Hill–Brownsville community's effort to empower themselves under these conditions.

Prelude to the 1966 Protests: Racial Segregation in New York City

The 1966 school year began with the opening of a new school, Intermediate School (I.S.) 201 in Harlem, and a parents' boycott. It was, at its opening, to be the first fully racially mixed New York school. The district superintendent reiterated that it would be integrated, but he now added that it would be 50 percent black and 50 percent Puerto Rican. Leaders of parent organizations and parents themselves, who had been difficult to rouse in the previous months, were now present, frustrated, and angry. Their representatives announced profoundly reformulated demands: The Board of Education was either to create mass integration immediately, that is, New York City schools that would be racially mixed and equally funded, or to turn inner city schools over to the control of their communities. It was clear to everyone present that a new struggle—the struggle for community control—had officially begun.[12]

Between 1960 and 1965, the city had made at least three separate supposed attempts to desegregate its schools. Early efforts during that period proved futile.[13] The ones that followed were even worse. All of these attempts had been responses to organized protest on the part of civil rights and parent groups. Although these organizations had made several sets of practical suggestions, what had forced the Board initially to move had been their two citywide boycotts. The first kept a half million black and Puerto Rican children and many thousands of white children out of school.[14] In the second, Malcolm X, Adam Clayton Powell, and Reverend Galamison had led the entire black school population over the Brooklyn Bridge to 110 Livingston Street, Board of Education headquarters. Representatives of the City Wide Committee for Integrated Schools, a coalition comprised of many advocacy groups, including the Parents' Workshop for Equality, the metropolitan branches of the National Association for the Advancement of Colored People (NAACP), the Committee on Racial Equality (CORE), the Harlem Parents' Committee, and the Urban League, saw demonstrations as means to an end. They hoped that the energy and vision generated by the Civil Rights movement could be used in its aftermath to routinize and systematize its initial aims.

Although the Board of Education had stated clearly that

there would be no "busing for integration," it was not clear what the alternatives were. Between 1950 and 1960, the city's racial and ethnic composition had changed dramatically. A net emigration of more than one million whites from the city had led to a 20 percent drop in white public school enrollment. Once 650,000 strong, there were now fewer than 500,000 white students in the New York City system. In the same period, there had been an influx into the city of nearly 400,000 African Americans and Latinos, which led, by 1960, to there being 600,000 black and Puerto Rican students in the New York City schools.[15]

New York City, like most American cities, was and is still highly segregated. Most blacks and Puerto Ricans lived with other blacks and Puerto Ricans in a few highly concentrated areas. Whites tended, if they were able, to live elsewhere.

One outcome of this demographic concentration was consistently overcrowded black and Puerto Rican classrooms. Indeed, in this period, several neighborhood schools had to create double sessions—that is, two separate school days in one in order to serve all of their students. The City Wide Committee observed that in nearby white schools, there were empty seats that could have accommodated many of these black students. Activist parents thus insisted again that schools would never be integrated without transfers and busing.[16]

The first transfer attempt was soon made. It brought five hundred children to Ridgewood and Glendale in Queens; several from East Harlem to Yorkville; and others from Williamsburg to Greenpoint. White reactions to the arrival of hundreds of black students in their communities were consistently negative, though most severe in Queens. There, a mob of irate citizens was ready to do whatever was necessary to keep the black third-graders from entering their schools. "Blacks go home!" was scrawled on school walls.[17] Some black parents insisted upon their children's continued attendance.

Members of this group, together with some parents from Queens, wrote a request asking that their respective all-white and all-black schools be paired. Superintendent Calvin Gross accepted their suggestion, the news of which brought fifteen thousand demonstrating white segregationists to City Hall, and announced his own Free Choice Transfer Plan. Gross was the first outsider to be appointed to the position of city superintendent. He was formerly chief of the Pittsburgh public school system. An opponent of involuntary busing, he assumed the position with popular support in 1963. Gross's transfer plan had promised a list of spaces in quality white schools—these were intended to be schools with buildings that were in decent shape, with sufficient quantities of school supplies, and with fairly low student-teacher ratios—that would be made available to black students who wished to be transferred out of their local districts. Integrationist leaders had assumed that there would be plenty of available spaces in the predominantly white schools. When the names of available schools were produced, however, there was much disappointment. Two of the schools with spaces to offer were across the city from Brooklyn, home to the majority of black students wishing to be transferred; another was a girls' school that had always been open to the black community; another already took a third of Brooklyn's black academic high school students; and the last was a predominantly white working-class school district in which white middle-class students falsified addresses to avoid assignment to their local school. What the Council had argued for, which none of these schools offered, was the bringing together of "good white" and "failing black" schools that existed next to one another.[18]

The second aim of the City Wide Committee was to end the new construction of segregated schools. As integrationist parents had mobilized, the Board of Education had attempted to deflect discontent by building new schools wherever protest movements had grown strong. These new buildings were accepted by the local districts; however, black and Puerto Rican parents disputed the sites that had been chosen for them. They demanded that the buildings be constructed on the residential fringes between black and white communities rather than at the center of predominantly black boroughs. Although the Board of Education formally agreed to this (they had also, after all, announced that the integration of schools within black communities seemed nearly impossible) their promises were soon forgotten. School zones were suddenly redrawn and plans made for the construction of 210 new schools to be built between 1965 and 1971. When building plans were made public in 1966, it was clear that 34 percent of these were guaranteed to be all black and/or Puerto Rican at the time of their opening; 28 percent would be all white. Segregated schools were to multiply by 400 percent, from 52 in 1954 to 201 in 1965. For every building site around which parents organized, ten new equally segregated schools passed smoothly through the budget. When attacked for hypocrisy, the Board claimed that it was only one of a number of organizations involved in the decision-making process. This was a true if impotent statement.[19]

Parent groups understood the logic of school construction and began to attend public hearings regarding each new school project. The work of Brooklyn parents focused primarily on what would become their local Junior High School 275. Each time a proposed site for the school came before the Board of Estimate, hundreds of parents arrived to picket, demonstrate, and demand integration. Their goal was to move the school site closer to or past the Linden Boulevard line. For in so doing, their school would also be school to the white community of Canarsie. A fringe site was at last chosen. As the center of a normal zoning circle, this promised fifty-fifty white-black student integration. Victory was hailed. Perhaps, the integrationist minority parents thought, past trends could be reversed. The school's opening three years later in 1962, however, dashed these hopes. In the intervening years, the Board had rezoned the site. It no longer included any white children. A massive and frustrating campaign followed. When the Board of Education incorporated two or three blocks of white Canarsie, producing a 70 rather than 100 percent black school, the white representatives of the white 30 percent went to court to reverse these motions. They argued, ironically, that considering race in zoning practices should have been outlawed. Although their first win was overturned in the Appellate Supreme Court, the school became an all black school through various transfer maneuvers. White children who lived a block away traveled a half mile each day to their predominantly white classrooms.[20]

Every meager move the Board made inspired immediate, dramatic, and often violent segregationist white response. The City Wide Committee led a third and final parent boycott. Demonstrators again demanded the improvement of ghetto schools, this time through total integration of junior high schools and the hiring of more black and Puerto Rican teachers. Very little changed, however. Superintendent Gross was replaced by Bernard Donovan, an attorney and anti-busing advocate. The Allen Plan—a proposal of the May 1964 Allen Report that was named after State Commissioner of Education James Allen Jr., and that demanded an affirmative effort at integration—was in the process of being postponed by the Board of Education. Parent involvement was low. Despite this, many middle-class organizations continued to participate consistently at Board of Education hearings. What had been a school integration movement with parents of color at its center appeared to be over. That is, until the opening of I.S. 201 in Harlem. A school boycott began in Harlem and spread quickly across the city through organizations that had been struggling together for half a decade. The tone and mood of these demonstrators and demonstrations were suddenly very different. The nature of the differences would soon become much clearer.

One of the new focal points was in Brooklyn. Blacks have lived in Brooklyn since the founding of the United States.[21] Indeed, they accounted for one in three borough residents in 1790. Although this percentage dropped considerably in the nineteenth and early twentieth centuries, by 1968, 39 percent of Brooklyn was black. This represented the largest proportion of blacks in the five boroughs of New York City. More important, perhaps, the majority of blacks in Brooklyn lived amongst other blacks. Although this borough combined people with loyalties to West Indian, southern, and northern black populations, this group combined, if not always easily or harmoniously, into racialized communities with common grievances. Nothing unified the community more than the aspiration for community empowerment and increased local control.

Ocean Hill had been part of the neighboring Bedford–Stuyvesant school district, with whose community struggles Ocean Hill's parents were actively involved. Each neighborhood had, depending on its size, a certain number of voting representatives on its district board. Ocean Hill had held one voting representative on the Bedford–Stuyvesant district board. Children in the Bedford–Stuyvesant district were allotted transfers to other districts as part of the city's integration plan. Four thousand Ocean Hill children, being part of the Bedford–Stuyvesant district, had been sent into white communities across the city in the midst of the Board of Education effort. Virtually all of these students had some form of bigotry and insult directed at them: Students at one school, for example, had been herded by their new principal into an all-black classroom of students bused from other parts of the city. Many could not keep up with the work and failed. Eventually, most children begged to be returned to their local schools. Their parents allowed most of them to do so. By September 1966, when most of them returned, their neighborhood was rezoned by the Board of Education into the new District 17, a district shared by Brownsville and East Flatbush. The catch in the new arrangement, however, was that Ocean Hill had no representation on the new district board.[22]

A group of community leaders immediately organized to protest Ocean Hill's lack of representation. Led by Father Powis, a white priest from Father of Our Lady Presentation Church, its central goal was to stimulate an almost inactive parents' association in the area. In November, it led the Ocean Hill community groups with which the Board of Education normally dealt in the cutting off of all relations with the District 17 Board and the central Board of Education. The demands for representation of community advocates had been snubbed. Local chapters of the UFT, the official union of New York teachers, provided local support for community groups. They saw in this collaboration a chance to ally against their own traditional enemy: the Board of Education. The configuration of political interests that brought these groups together were soon to shift.

At the same time, a group of teachers in the Ocean Hill area, recognizing their own school as the unnamed prototypical problem school in a newspaper story on Ocean Hill, called the UFT headquarters to ask for help in ridding their junior high school of its principal. They were encouraged to work with local parents. When these two groups picketed together at the District Superintendent's office, they not only were given a commitment that the principal would be removed, but were awarded additional services for their school, including relief for chronic overcrowding. Surprised by this victory, the group realized that, if well organized, they might be able to receive permission from the Board of Education to design new programs and participate in the designation of the new administration at their school that was soon to become I.S. 55.[23] Various community groups met regularly during the fall and throughout the winter. According to Richard Karp, "They discussed the chronic problems of the ghetto school: lack of discipline, on the one hand, and on the other, the suspensions of students—the latter a sore point to the parents of Ocean Hill, who had seen large numbers of their young ejected onto the streets without diplomas."[24]

In January 1967, Father Powis's group of activists and the group of I.S. 55 teachers merged, calling themselves "The Steering Committee for I.S. 55." Together they drew up a proposal that would incorporate the community into the processes of selecting the new principal and drawing up the new school's program through creating provisions for an elected governing board and for educational improvements. Their work drew heavily on the Gottsfeld-Gordon plan, a proposal that Harry Gottsfeld and Sol Gordon of Yeshiva University were developing for I.S. 201.[25]

Commentators disagree over the degree and kind of power that the combined groups sought. Diane Ravitch insists that the plan itself was one designed to enable community participation, not control; it proposed an elected governing board, but one with limited functions rather than the power to hire and fire school employees.[26] Similarly, Eugenia Kemble suggests that the enthusiasm of teachers for the project was precisely due to their belief that they might be instrumental in assuring that education programs, like "learning centers" and the "More Effective Schools Program," would supplement the new administrative format.[27] Highly focused on their own school, teachers hoped that with new programs would come, among other things, specialists, schoolwide parent-teacher councils, and adult education.

In a different vein, Richard Karp argued that the community's proposal implied direct community control and a corresponding end to the Board of Education's long-held power over the nine hundred schools and one million students comprising the New York City school system.[28] Furthermore, he suggested that when Father Powis met with Mario Fantini, a former school teacher and administrator and representative of the Ford Foundation, to discuss making an experimental district out of eight schools, including I.S. 55, in Ocean Hill–Brownsville, and to solicit Fantini's aid in procuring Ford Foundation funding for the project, he expressed a fundamental lack of faith in the power of the education system to reform itself. He argued that the funding the foundation soon offered was an effort to help actualize community control.[29]

It is highly likely, however, that feelings within the combined teacher-community group were highly varied, as are all collaborations of organizations working for community participation in institutions that have previously made it superfluous. Because efforts to effectively involve communities in the running of schools had been marginal up to this point, the significance of the difference in measures advocated to accomplish this aim would only become clearer as more varied efforts were tried. It was already evident, though, that the approaches advocated by the teachers were focused primarily on the expansion of programs, while Powis's cohort was concerned with administrative control and procedures employed in the discipline of local students. One thing that the conflict soon clarified were the different kinds of power required by communities seeking to be effectively involved in the administration of their schools. At this stage, it was not as obvious. Either way, their proposal clearly incorporated protections of teachers' rights, as outlined by the UFT. In the new administrative arrangements, an impartial review of any substantive

charges against a teacher was to be carried out by a board—
consisting of a college professor, a public school teacher, and a
community person—appointed by the governing board.

Ravitch has argued that members of the Board of
Education had themselves become interested in the possibility
of administrative decentralization, and that they approached
the Ford Foundation in search of support.[30] Others disagree,
arguing that the initial impetus came clearly from the foundation itself. Ford, the argument goes, sought to experiment
with its own educational theories and was in need of a community to serve as a laboratory.[31] Still others suggest that it
was in fact the mayor and city government who had much to
do with the beginnings. Whether out of fear of continued
civic disruption and a feeble response to citywide demands for
law and order, an effort to stabilize a system through absorb-
ing dissidence, a scheme to undercut the growing power of
the UFT, to transfer accountability for ongoing school failure
away from the central Board, or an attempt to increase its
budget for educational purposes, the administration of Mayor
John Lindsay had reacted eagerly to demands for citizen participation.

In February 1967, the city Board of Education approved
the proposal for the experimental district "in concept" and the
Ford Foundation made a grant of $44,000 to Father Powis's
church. This money was "to cover preparation for elections,
efforts to involve parents and other residents more in school
affairs, training institutes for governing board members and
community school workers, educational consultants, and budgetary specialists."[32] A planning council was to be selected for
the operation of the demonstration project. The Board of
Education moved quickly. On April 19, it produced its Policy
on Decentralization. This was a plan, if a vague one, for citywide decentralization and greater community participation in
the schools. Although it was less than satisfactory to members

of the local board, the policy on decentralization recommended sweeping changes, including provision for certain experimental districts.

The mayor advocated the creation of thirty to sixty new autonomous boards that were to be elected almost entirely by parents. A minority of the membership would still be appointed by the mayor. These local boards, together with district superintendents and principals were to have increased administrative responsibilities including final authority over the budget, curriculum, and personnel at their district schools. The Board of Examiners, an agency designed to regulate the civil service qualification would be abolished; state standards for school personnel were to suffice. These changes, argued the mayor's office, were needed to maximize the balance between flexibility and authority at the local level with centralized standards. Through the creation of experimental units, the Board hoped to achieve greater community involvement. The specific design of these experiments had not yet been decided. Some of the ideas included: dividing single districts into two, each with its own board and superintendent; setting up within a school board area small groupings of schools including primary, intermediate, and high schools with contracted services with a university; establishing a small district in which parents and community representatives would work more centrally in school programs and in the development of new approaches to teacher training and curriculum development; and creating a series of demonstrations in single schools involving parents centrally in the project of strengthening early childhood education and improvement in the instruction of fundamentals. (The experiment in Ocean Hill–Brownsville later tried to implement elements of all of these.) The Board here welcomed any proposals and suggestions.[33]

Mayor Lindsay, who had been directed by the state legislature to prepare a complete decentralization plan by the end of the year, sought assistance from the president of the Ford Foundation, McGeorge Bundy. Together they hoped to expand the terms of this original plan into one that ceded considerably more power to community-based boards. But this was still in the works.

Summer of 1967: The Elections, The Proposal, and The Beginnings of Sharp Division

The planning council for Ocean Hill–Brownsville, made up of parents and community leaders who had participated in the Steering Committee for I.S. 55, was to begin its work that summer. Teacher members had been elected at each school to serve for the summer only. As they understood it, faculties at each school would vote on whether to be part of the project as devised at the opening of the fall term.

The council appointed Rhody McCoy as its acting unit administrator. The acting principal of a "600" school in Manhattan, McCoy had come to Ocean Hill–Brownsville to interview for the job of principal at I.S. 55. A "600" school is a school earmarked by the number 600 to designate its low status of achievement in the system.[34]

Born in 1923, the son of a postal employee, McCoy had grown up in Washington, D.C. After earning degrees from Howard and New York Universities, he started his career in New York City in 1949. A soft-spoken man and father of seven, McCoy could negotiate the public school bureaucracy with consummate skill. Although he had risen slowly through its hierarchy, McCoy had been passed over several times for promotion in favor of white, Jewish administrators whom he thought were less competent than he. He felt that the school system benefitted its white staff more than its students.[35]

Unlike the black leaders who dominated early 1960s' media coverage of the Civil Rights movement, McCoy had long advocated the philosophy of Malcolm X over that of Martin Luther King Jr. He frequently traveled to X's house for long discussions. His hope was that the Ocean Hill–Brownsville experiment would be the first step toward a black-run and black-controlled school system stretching from elementary school through college.[36]

During the summer, the planning council held several meetings with Superintendent Donovan and his staff in order to clarify their work and the distinction between decentralization and community control. During this time, the council began to confer with a variety of consultants, especially persons connected with Brooklyn College and Queens College to help them with revising the Ford Foundation proposal and supervising the election of the local board. They would rely on these connections increasingly in the coming year. The original proposal to the Ford Foundation and the Board of Education called for the election of a local governing board comprised of one parent from each school.

The campaign began on July 5, 1967. Trouble began when the council approached the Board of Education in need of files with the names and addresses of students. They needed to register those parents who were eligible to vote. Board representatives told them that they would need to hire two of the Board's secretaries to acquire this information. When community representatives promptly agreed, they were told that these secretaries had in fact gone on vacation and that no one else was available to help. As a result, some 2,200 prospective voters were registered in a door-to-door campaign led by nuns from Father Powis's church, poverty workers, and paid parent-canvassers.[37] As registration information was collected, sheets detailing the project plan were distributed. Parents were asked for signatures attesting that the program had been explained to them and to indicate their approval or disapproval of the experimental concept. There was also a petition inviting parents to nominate candidates to the governing board. Posters, newspaper ads, flyers, radio advertisements, television broadcasts, mass meetings, and church notices announced the August 4 election day. For many members of the community, this would be their first voting experience. Sixty-one candidates were nominated.

Eleven hundred people came to the individual schools, where police cadets and students from Brooklyn College were conducting and supervising the vote. In the two days that followed, parents who had not shown up were canvassed in their homes. Much attention was paid to questions about the legitimacy of this local election. One widely quoted onlooker, noting the absence of an accredited agency like the Honest Ballot Association, said that the procedures had been "unorthodox, but considered by observers to be an honest effort to obtain the votes of all parents." She continued, "Although the cardboard boxes and desk drawers that were pressed into service as ballot boxes could easily have been opened and tampered with, no charges were made or misdeeds observed." She concluded, "There was no evidence of coercion during the nominating process or during the election period itself."[38]

The Niemeyer Committee, chaired by then president of Bank Street School of Education, Dr. John H. Niemeyer, which the Board of Education had appointed to monitor and evaluate the system's overall decentralization plan, had expected the Ocean Hill–Brownsville planning council to devote the summer to the planning process alone. It was "suddenly confronted with the fact that an election was in full swing."[39] The council's proposal had not formally included an election. It had, however, stated that the governing board would be ready to take office in early August 1967.

Ravitch, doing historical work later, pointed out critically that thirteen of the twenty paid canvassers in the August election had also been candidates.[40] Of these thirteen, five were

parent-association presidents. She claimed that these irregu-
larities, along with the haste of the elections, later informed
criticism on the part of union teachers, who argued that the
election had been, in Ravitch's words, "... a deliberate vehicle
to transform the self-appointed board into the elected governing board."[41] The governing board defended itself from these
charges, arguing that there had been no ready-made guidelines available to them. They had, if anything, been encouraged by the high rates of participation. The question of
acceptable guidelines, however, or the governing board's concern that these needed to be reformulated, would reemerge
repeatedly in the following year.

In any event, seven parent members were elected to the
governing board. They, in turn, chose five community leaders.
The list included two clergymen, one assemblyman, a community center director, and a Puerto Rican poverty aide. Reverend C. Herbert Oliver, who had not played a role in the
original Steering Committee, was named board chairman.

The final proposal of the experimental board, which was
to be implemented in 1968, was ready in late August. It began
with a tone of foreboding. Wrote McCoy:

> [M]en are capable of putting an end to what they find
> intolerable without recourse to politics. As history has so
> frequently recorded, the ending of oppression and the
> beginning of a new day has often become a reality only
> after a people have resorted to violent means. [42]

People in Ocean Hill–Brownsville, he said, had been "at
such a point of desperation" when the project was authorized.
The experiment therefore represented "the last threads of the
community's faith in the school system's purposes and abilities."[43] The document then included results of the election, a
proposal that McCoy be made the project administrator, and

the candidates for that position requested by the Board. It claimed that the governing board was answerable to the New York City superintendent and the state commissioner of education in all matters pertaining to the schools and that it was within the body's power to appoint a business manager, nominees for community-relations liaison, and community school workers. The governing board further claimed the right to recommend and select the project administrator, to approve selected principals, to determine policy in areas of curriculum, professional-personnel conditions, and generally in matters concerning the program at large; to determine its own budgetary needs and the allocation of its funds, and to apply directly for extended funding. Finally, the governing board argued that they, rather than the Board of Education, would make provisions for evaluations of the project.[44]

This draft of the plan differed somewhat from the one used to secure the Ford grant. It no longer included its formal teachers' protection clause. The methods for selecting the project administrator and principals in the case of vacancies had been changed. And the request that Ocean Hill–Brownsville schools be given More Effective School (MES) status and the other supplementary programs that accompanied it had been abandoned. According to Maurice Goldbloom, the MES program

> ... was based on the use of a whole battery of remedial services in particular schools in ghetto areas; the ratio of pupils to staff is approximately 12 to 1 as compared to its city-wide ratio of about 16 to 1.[45]

In her history of this controversy, Diane Ravitch noted that there was "... nothing mentioned about the power to hire, fire, or transfer professionals. Nor was there any educational proposal, as there had been in the original plan approved in the spring ... nor were there any bylaws for the new board."[46] The document *was* very vague. Yet it could, arguably, incorporate the powers Ravitch has identified as absent through the more general guidelines that gave the governing board authority to appoint business managers and approve selected principals, both of whom would be professionals with those powers.

Deterioration of the Relationship between the Governing Board and the UFT Teachers

Upon reading the proposal for the governing board's powers to direct the affairs of the upcoming school year, teachers were concerned and angry. Teacher representatives had voiced objections over the summer regarding the possibility of teachers being evaluated by the governing board. The clause directly concerning them had been revised to say that the board would not be doing the evaluations that would determine tenure or promotion, but this did not assuage the teachers' concerns. An earlier draft had suggested that the governing board would hire a separate agency to consider charges made against teachers. Teachers had expressed fears that high concentrations of power were accumulating at the local level. This might not have been a problem if relations had been better between the teachers and the governing board up to this point. Instead they had begun to deteriorate much earlier, before the campaign and election had started.

The local board had raised questions about the role of teachers in reform early in the process. Although they had worked with teachers whom they believed to be sensitive to the needs of the community and aware of the ineffectual efforts of many of their colleagues, teacher participation in the running of the experiment would place them in an awkward role "since," reflected McCoy, "[they] belong[ed] to the system on which [they had to] turn."[47] Other members of the board argued that if teachers were willing to play this role, they would lend sophistication and stability to the project and would bring union support.[48] The failure to work this out had much broader implications than the local board initially expected.

Harriet Goldstein, a local UFT chapter chairman and teacher representative to the board, claimed that the original budget attached to the Ford Foundation proposal had been removed in copies given to the teachers on the Steering Committee. It had allotted $10,000 for publicity and preparation for the elections, $5,000 as "innovative allowance" for the board, $5,000 for matters of contingency, $5,260 for a governing board and community-school workers' institute, and money to be paid to participants in training sessions at $15 per time. The remainder was to cover any invited speakers, typists, bookkeepers, accountants, and other personnel.[49] This financial plan clearly revealed a commitment less to programs like MES than to those central to the internal restructuring and creating of a community institution. It should be borne in mind that such a budget was proposed in 1967 to initiate a structure for further development. The $44,000 they ended up receiving from the Ford Foundation was seen as a meager amount. Leaders of the demonstration project had hoped to receive five million dollars from the foundation so that they could hire two hundred members of the Ocean Hill–Brownsville community as full-time employees of the experiemental school district.

Most teacher representatives to the summer planning council had been appointed by their respective faculties at the close of the prior school year. They had indicated that they would spend the summer in New York City and that they were interested in participating in the experiment. They had been given a set of expectations outlined by the planning council;

these required that they fully participate in all phases of planning, exhibit confidence in other participants, show faith in the potential of the project, contribute honestly to all discussion, involve themselves in consensus decision-making procedures, maintain professional standards, be focused around the primary objective of improving education, and show accountability to all interested parties.[50]

Meetings with teachers, the Steering Committee, and community residents were organized by a "summer coordinator." Impasses soon emerged around issues of teacher representation on the board; teacher responsibility to the board; supervision, tenure, and evaluation; voting; and the legality of the decentralization operation. By the end of the summer, the discontent of teachers had intensified. They argued that the standards of behavior as laid out by the board had not been met by the board; that they had not been included in the process of choosing the unit administrator; they had not been informed of all meetings; that the final plan they had expected to help rewrite was reworked without them; and that all the objections they had made to particular ideas led to the disputed portions being dropped rather than revised.[51] The teachers recalled that other participants on the council had contributed to a "constant stream of remarks ... which stated that teachers were bigoted, incompetent, uninterested, obstructive, and [that they] were attempting to sabotage the plan."[52] Others said that "the atmosphere became so hostile that teachers hesitated even to ask a question or express an opinion. Any attempt at teacher comment was met with insults or charges of obstruction."[53] Needless to say, the concept of consensus decision-making had been dropped.

Teachers claimed repeatedly that they had not been allowed to vote. They had not been a part of choosing McCoy and had been barred from the elections of parent representatives. McCoy said that these restrictions had been due to teachers' attempts to "see that no militant or Black Power advocates were selected. This to us was an attempt to exclude a vital segment of the community and to deny the exercise of free choice."[54]

All of this was intensified when McCoy underscored his lack of interest in anxieties expressed by district teachers by nominating Herman Ferguson for the position of principal at I.S. 55. Ferguson had been indicted two months earlier for conspiring to murder moderate civil rights leaders Roy Wilkins and Whitney Young. His outspoken opposition to the MES program made him even less favorable to the UFT. His selection in Ocean Hill–Brownsville was believed to confirm some teachers' fear about the militancy of the unit administrator and their own prospects as white teachers in a black district. A member of the governing board told reporters that Ferguson was "not afraid of changes from old methods of teaching," and was "the person to keep teachers in line."[55] Teachers, already seeing the board as heavy-handed, did not think that they needed to take special measures to keep employees "in line."[56] The idea of Ferguson as the potential man to do it was repugnant to them.

Superintendent Donovan, the State Education Department, and the Niemeyer Committee were also against the appointment of Ferguson. While they accepted the other three nominations for principals, on August 30, they asked McCoy to withdraw his name. McCoy reported these events to his board saying:

> This I refused and was supported by Reverend Oliver. There was much discussion by all present from reasons to legality. Reverend Oliver stated, "No one had the right to judge or determine the guilt or innocence of the candidate. Since he was still a Board of Education employee, we were within our rights to consider him." This was agreed but it was requested that his name still

be removed because of the publicity and the feelings of Superintendent Donovan and the Board. Reverend Oliver stated that too often a minority member was accused, tried, and sentenced by the press or public opinion before the trial and in most cases damaging to the person who may have been found innocent.[57]

When the nominations were put to the local board vote the next day, teachers argued adamantly against Ferguson. They feared that his selection would encourage bad publicity for the project and urged that the board delay the vote until later that fall. When it was time to vote, the teachers abstained. The other members of the governing board voted unanimously for Ferguson. The abstention infuriated the other members of the board who only became more angry when the same teachers later claimed that they had not been allowed to vote. Perhaps this was ultimately irrelevant, for the Board of Education acted on their behalf and finally refused Ferguson.[58]

At the newly elected governing board's August 31, 1967 meeting, the board had to vote for the retention or replacement of Rhody McCoy as unit administrator. At this meeting, teachers from Ocean Hill–Brownsville suddenly nominated a white principal, Jack Bloomfield of Junior High School (J.H.S.) 271, for the job. Bloomfield was also the Board's preferred candidate. The Board's support was bad enough, but the governing board especially resented the teachers' action. They saw it as "a symbolic gesture of 'no confidence' in their unit administrator's leadership."[59] Hurt feelings were one thing; what followed was worse. Bloomfield, feeling that it would be unwise to stay in Ocean Hill–Brownsville and that his failure to leave would lead to a division at the level of leadership, requested to be transferred out of the district. The Board refused this request, however. When Bloomfield finally left six months later, he took most of the employees of his school with him.

In the midst of all of this, a citywide teacher's strike loomed. The Board of Education and the UFT had not yet reached settlement on a contract. One of the central demands was that measures be taken to provide stricter controls over disruptive children. Civil rights organizations, representatives of the Ocean Hill–Brownsville community, and most black teachers opposed this proposal. Their goal was to create the structures that would lead to mass improvements in the educational performance of students of color. From their perspective, "the union was preparing to strike for the power to put black and Puerto Rican children out of class more easily."[60] The UFT approached the local board supposedly offering them a deal: In exchange for support for their strike, the UFT would stand behind the demonstration project. In retrospect this offer could only have been disingenuous. The UFT had opposed every decentralization bill submitted up to this point. And the Ocean Hill–Brownsville governing board went beyond decentralization to community control, a more radical version of the infrastructural shifts the union opposed. Parents in the demonstration project had already determined that in the event of a 1967 strike, they would keep their schools open. Ravitch argued that project leaders now saw themselves as autonomous employers and wanted to begin the year by exercising their new role.[61] Her negative appraisal, however, overlooked the support that most black and some white teachers offered for this decision. Local board members wanted their schools open for the start of the new semester; they were trying to cultivate parent support through the offer of new possibilities, so what would closings prove? What is more, the governing board hoped that with their extended control, issues like the disruptive child issue would no longer be articulated in such racially encoded terms. When the governing board refused the UFT offer, however, the teachers' union representatives, despite some rank and file support for the local governing board, joined in the chorus that "extremism" and "Black Power would prevail in these communities."[62]

The Opening of the 1967 to 1968 School Year

At the opening of the school year, eighteen assistant principals and five principals requested transfers out of Ocean Hill–Brownsville.[63] Governing board members visited each school in order to recapitulate the events of the summer. Teachers did not want to listen, however. Perhaps sparked by the UFT's planning council summer representatives or by the UFT's leadership itself, faculties in the Ocean Hill–Brownsville district now objected. There was open resentment to parental control. Teachers charged that there had been a Black Power takeover of their schools. All of the changes had been effected through undemocratic processes. The Ocean Hill–Brownsville conflict became a cause célèbre among teachers citywide, and it fed into the general strike fever. Almost with a sense of vindictiveness, the strike began on September 1967.

In terms of power, the union had recently come of age. Earlier in 1967, the UFT had won the right to write school policy into its contract. Albert Shanker was the organization's elected head since 1964. A tough, Old Left unionist and anti-Communist, Shanker was born into a poor Jewish family in Long Island in 1928. He attended the New York public schools, the University of Illinois, and Columbia University, and had begun teaching junior high school mathematics in 1952 when he became active in the New York Teachers' Guild, the forerunner to the UFT.[64] The Guild became the UFT in November 1960.

Many observers saw the fall strike as a turning point that reformulated the conflict in Ocean Hill–Brownsville as a white-black power struggle.[65] Black teachers in District 17 schools supported the governing board's efforts to keep the schools open. Black teachers from other parts of the city also came to the demonstration schools to assist.

Parents in Ocean Hill–Brownsville had already made plans to staff the school in the event of a strike. "All efforts to convince them that they should open only three or four of the seven schools were to no avail," said McCoy. Even the suggestion that the schools be open only a half day was vetoed. "They were determined to give evidence to all that they had accepted the challenge and would assume full responsibility."[66] Parents participated in many teacher-training sessions conducted by local teachers, members of the African-American Teachers Association, and Herman Ferguson. Community members commented that the strike served to solidify segments of the community, as parents worked with their children and observed once again the substandard conditions under which the learning process was supposed to take place.[67]

The governing board had already begun to see that their chief and most immediate hindrance would be the union. The strike made it clear that white teachers' loyalty was primarily with the UFT. Unlike the majority of their black colleagues, they looked there rather than to the governing board for legitimacy and authority. Although none of the planning council's proposals had specifically requested the right to hire and fire employees, they, now local leaders, became convinced that it would be a necessary precondition for community control.

Wrote Richard Karp, "After the strike, the teachers who returned to Ocean Hill–Brownsville did so with bitterness and were met by [a community who felt an equal sense of bitterness]."[68] Several schools were effectively torn apart by antagonisms between the white teachers who felt the community leadership was unsympathetic to their concerns and black teachers and parents who saw the strike as a clear sign of opposition to community control.[69]

While the local board struggled to assert their authority, the UFT joined with the New York City Council of Supervisory Associations (CSA) to try to prevent the district from picking their principals from outside the regular civil service channels. After the departure of most of the schools' former administrators, Superintendent Donovan had appointed an ad hoc committee to devise job descriptions that might help to procure new administrators. The committee's standards went beyond the regular job experiences of principals in that it required a specific New York State certificate or license to teach; graduate or undergraduate courses in community organizing, urban education, or urban social planning; two years of teaching or supervision in a disadvantaged area or special service school; and one hundred hours of non-compensated service in school, youth, or community activities in the demonstration area or one like it.[70] The UFT and the CSA now sued to void appointments that had been made through use of these alternative guidelines. Some suggest that this was purely the UFT's retribution. Others argued that it was another example of its fears of decentralization and its belief that these changes in guidelines of hiring clearly denied the merit of already employed principals.[71] They saw this disregard for bureaucratic procedure as a symbolic strike at the union's most precious and hard-won job security.[72] Despite pending charges, the Board of Education allowed the governing board to retain the principals they had already hired. It refused the local board's request for permission to hire its own assistant principals without regard to existing lists, however. Although these positions were also being vacated, the state commissioner of education advised that all decisions of the kind be postponed pending the outcome of the court challenge.[73]

As far as the governing board was concerned, the UFT's hostility was damaging the project's potential for success.

McCoy initiated a series of meetings with Shanker, hoping to resolve some differences. It was not clear to anyone involved whether this was possible. Still, their private meetings culminated in the creation of a committee of teachers within the district to prepare proposals for new programs.[74]

Few Ocean Hill–Brownsville teachers understood the goals or intentions of the governing board. At a December meeting that brought the teachers, McCoy, and the governing board together, teachers asked many questions. Among them were: "There is a black-white split in the schools in your district. What are you going to do as Unit Administrator to correct this problem?" "Do you want to have an entirely Afro-American staff in the schools in our district?" "What have you done to get parents to participate?" "There has been a rumor that your policy has been influenced by an outside militant group. Is this true?"[75] Although discussion helped somewhat, it could not resolve all misunderstandings. It seemed that as two separate bodies, the teachers and the board, had diametrically opposed interests.

These internal problems were exacerbated by external difficulties with the Board of Education. The local governing board had refused the guidelines outlined for it by an advisory committee to the board in December. Ocean Hill–Brownsville representatives insisted that their unit administrator would be responsible solely to their local board; that they should be able to apply for outside funding, bypassing standard Board of Education procedures; and that they wanted the process of outside evaluation to begin in September 1968 rather than 1967. Project lawyers, hired by Queens College, also reiterated requests that had been overlooked entirely by the Advisory Committee: local control over the budget, including the right to intermingle funds; freedom to establish a curriculum subject to state rather than city standards, including the right to purchase directly their own textbooks and supplies; and the right to establish at least one demonstration project training school, with the result that the selection of personnel from it could avoid normal procedures.[76]

These demands created difficulties for the Board of Education. It could not legally delegate these powers, even if its members wished to do so. The Board's formal and repeated commitment was to gradual change. Members felt that they had already fulfilled their duties to the project by allowing the local board to function without formal recognition, by appointing the nominees of the governing board to principalships (except for Ferguson), by rejecting challenges to the idea of the district experiment within their own communities, and by appealing the ruling against the appointment of "demonstration principals" without removing those already hired.[77] Furthermore, when McCoy had fought for the money to finance his own staff, the Board had granted him a lump sum budget to do so.

From the perspective of the governing board, however, the Board of Education and its staff had consistently blocked their efforts. Checks for district employees who were not on the regular payroll were delayed for months, and McCoy was running his office out of an unheated storefront. Some of the board's complaints were the effects of bureaucratic inefficiency. Others did grow out of genuine hostility to the local board and its aims. Of more concern than any of these matters, however, the governing board had sensed what it would need to make their schools work for local children, and their claims were now being denied. What, after all, was a broken rule, if breaking it would further their aims? What was recognition without power? What were principals without the ability to control their staff? What was more, without formal recognition from the Board of Education, the Ford Foundation could not continue to fund the project.

While the Board of Education continued to meet with the

governing board in the effort to come to terms that would allow for the grant of formal recognition, the situation between many white and black teachers, as well as between many of the white teachers and the governing board, worsened. In one teachers' cafeteria, black teachers sat on one side while white teachers sat on the other.[78] Communication between them was "at best polite, more often curt, and most of the time nonexistent."[79] To the black teachers, their white counterparts were on a mission to destroy local control. It was often said that white teachers were working for the UFT and not the children, that white teachers were "letting the students run wild to discredit the program," and that "the white community [always said] Negroes [had] no pride or ambition, when some pride and ambition [were shown], they [would] do everything they [could] to suppress it."[80]

"Absenteeism" on the part of white teachers was the most common complaint. One day a black teacher reported that twenty-eight teachers were out "sick" from one school alone.[81] Another account, which became a cause célèbre, told of a white teacher pouring paint on a classroom floor. She allegedly said that she planned to "blame it on a Black student as proof of riot and insurrection in the community."[82] It is obviously difficult to substantiate these stories thirty years after the fact. What is clear, though, is that they express the profound frustration and anger of black teachers in response to white. White teachers publicly and commonly said that they were in favor of community control, but they disputed the ability of the people in Ocean Hill–Brownsville to carry out the work.[83] Some said residents were not "educated" or "socially-elevated enough to run schools," that they should have achieved middle-class status before participating in such a project. Others said the same thing in more subtle garb: that they would be more willing to accept a governing board if it were made up of representatives of the church, the business world, and influential organizations like the NAACP or the Urban League.[84] The majority of white union teachers in the city believed in labor unionism and the "idea that society's problems would and should be solved by centralized boards of experts and professionals."[85] Needless to say, these sentiments, whether the white teachers recognized it or not, were repugnant to a poor community seeking some influence over their local failing schools.

McCoy encountered this deep ideological divide in countless mundane ways. He found resentment of the concept on the part of the supervisory personnel manifested in "lapses of memory, the need for clarification of standard practices, inability to respond to directives, interruption of schedules, and many other omissions."[86] Accusations of assault and hostility were abundant. Rumors spread and mushroomed into grossly distorted charges of racism. McCoy reflected that although key people in the community were perceptive enough to employ (or devise) "diversionary tactics to soften the impact" of attacks from all sides, the governing board had not developed a publicity committee or a process whereby only selected people would publicly discuss the project.[87] This meant that the public heard honest and sincere feelings on the part of the community. Because many of these comments were angry, it also allowed critics to capitalize on them.

In the midst of all this McCoy was trying to run a new, experimental school district. In addition to biweekly meetings, the governing board established communication, information, and public relations centers within the community. Board members held community meetings, attended Parent-Teacher Association (PTA) sessions, and spoke on invitation to a variety of audiences interested in the project. They formed a curriculum and bylaws committee; they selected new principals; they directed attention to the opening of the new I.S. 55; they held meetings with college representatives to discuss potential new programs and affiliations; they placed student teachers and welcomed their supervisors; and they enlisted parent volunteers to try to establish paraprofessional training programs. They spent innumerable hours interpreting the program to the community and dedicated even more time to helping principals ascertain school needs. McCoy tried, to the extent that he was able, to determine the basis for the many requests for transfer made by assistant principals. He also realized that support from teachers often increased in direct proportion to the opportunities they had to ask questions and to eliminate misunderstanding. McCoy and his staff made efforts to be as professional as possible without promising to deliver what they were not capable of doing or providing. This balance proved difficult, however, for the limits and possibilities of their powers remained unresolved. In March, the governing board's request to change existing procedures for the hiring of new assistant principals had been overridden by the superintendent of schools and the state commissioner of education after being contested by the New York City Council of Supervisory Associations (CSA). They were thus forced to take assistant principals from the existing civil service list according to their numerical rating without consideration of subject competence or the extent to which they could complement or provide meaningful resources to the existing staff. The superintendent of schools and the state commissioner, however, allowed McCoy to recruit his own district superintendent staff. Representatives of the state wished repeatedly to discuss the qualifications of the staff. McCoy was sure that the real purpose of these meetings was to determine candidates' affiliations or degrees of militancy.

An attorney hired by the Community Studies Program at Queens College, Howard Kalodner, explained that the impasse between the governing board and their opponents was an outgrowth of different conceptions of the experiment itself.[88] The

Board of Education had wished to experiment with the idea of decentralization across the whole system and thus was not willing to give the local board any powers greater than those held by district superintendents. The governing board, on the other hand, believed that their district had been given community control. Why, they thought, would a district in such dire condition be used to experiment with bureaucratic decentralization when the solution was so obvious? McCoy and his colleagues hoped to make the school into a community institution generating the structures through which to develop a genuine community among the residents of Ocean Hill– Brownsville. Local children would be at the center of the educational project and would be in regular and sustained contact with thoughtful and mature adult models of their own background. All of this would cohere around job opportunities and contacts that could be deliberately put in the service of improving the economy of the surrounding neighborhood.[89] In order to do this, they would need funds to carry out these reforms and the power to hire and dismiss personnel.

In April 1968, McCoy wrote that black educators

> ... must become the vital force in halting the downward trend in urban education. The tokenism which we now endure must develop into a rampaging conflagration that will ultimately mean control. The policymakers and first-line implementors of the educational process for black and Puerto Rican children must be black and Puerto Rican educators. ... The reform movement in education will raise the aspirations of the black community all over the country to the point where violence will be the unquestionable consequence of denial. ... Whites cannot prepare fast enough to cope with the determination and commitment of those of us who are pledged to wrest from their illegal hold on the future of ourselves and our

children. If whites are not willing to relinquish this stranglehold, if they are not willing to work with Blacks in resolving these Herculean problems, then the battle lines are drawn. There will be massive, persistent, and even violent confrontations.[90]

Many believed that the Board of Education was waiting for the Ocean Hill board to "wither away in bitter impotence," for in the midst of political gridlock, angry and frustrated parents' groups demanded action from the local board.[91] The local board finally announced that if the Board of Education did not accept its outlines of community control in ten days, it would resign.

There was no movement. While representatives of the experimental district said that they would oppose any decentralizing legislation because such legislation did not necessarily mean community control—since a decentralized district could still be in the hands of professionals from outside of the community—political support for a strong decentralization bill was elsewhere on the rise. A bill sponsored by the State Board of Regents advocated the division of the city into fifteen regular school districts. Each was to have maximum autonomy, subject only to the limited supervision of a new five-member Board of Education. The bill also provided for the creation of a limited number of "target districts," in which state certification rather than the requirements of the Board of Examiners would serve as minimum qualification for new personnel. Although Mayor Lindsay was in full support of this proposal, the adjournment-minded legislature remained unmoved. They instead enacted a weaker decentralization bill sponsored by State Senator Marchi, which would delay the issue for another year.

The UFT, Council of Supervisory Associations (CSA), and factions within the Board of Education opposed all of these suggested measures. They saw them as a direct attack on the common school system and as based in a romanticization of a decentralized past in which, in actuality, local political bosses had run schools according to their political interests alone. They believed that centralization had been the only effective remedy; that egalitarian policy had only ever emanated from the state, federal, or municipal level.[92] Integration, one of their shared official commitments, could not be achieved in a decentralized system.

At a meeting in the beginning of May, in which representatives of the Board of Education sought the local board's support for their next legislative move, a representative of the local board asked, "What happens if the governing board wants teachers to leave but they want to remain?" Deputy Superintendent Brown explained that the board would have to bring charges such as "incompetence, insubordination, etc." Governing board members asked what would happen if conditions were made sufficiently uncomfortable that a teacher might wish to transfer; Dr. Brown pointed out that "the UFT contract and its provision for grievance procedures might not allow that."[93]

On May 10, 1968, the Ocean Hill–Brownsville board peremptorily transferred thirteen teachers, two of them UFT chapter chairmen, five assistant principals, and one principal to central headquarters for reassignment. The Ocean Hill–Brownsville board decided that those being transferred were sabotaging the project. The union quickly branded the transfers "firings."[94] Superintendent Donovan ordered the nineteen to ignore the board's order and return to their schools. When they did so, on Monday, May 13, parents blockaded the entrances to the schools. Police surrounded the buildings and threatened to escort the ousted teachers through the blockade. They made no actual move to do so.

When a larger number of police officers appeared on May 15 and proceeded to admit all "authorized personnel," the governing board refused to assign duties to the returning teachers, assistant principals, and the principal. The UFT demanded that the nineteen be given due process hearings and struck the Ocean Hill–Brownsville schools for the remainder of the year. Teacher boycotts were countered by parent counter boycotts. Black parents charged racism and police brutality. They were in turn accused by picketting teachers and UFT supporters of "vigilantism" and black racism.[95]

Superintendent Donovan and the Board of Regents again began to pressure the legislature to pass a strong decentralization bill. Legislative leaders agreed to work on such a plan. A group of decentralization advocates among them threatened civil action if a plan were not quickly adopted.

On May 21, Governor Rockefeller predicted proudly that a strong bill would soon be passed in Albany. At the time, however, he was not aware of the significance of the events that had transpired the day before. Albert Shanker and five hundred New York City school teachers had arrived in the capitol city to lobby against the impending legislation.[96]

3

White Power

The Construction of Jews as the Voice of Reason

A sort of hoodlum element is in control of several schools.... Teachers remaining in Ocean Hill–Brownsville are subject to a kind of vigilante activity.... Children in Ocean Hill–Brownsville are chanting Black Power slogans.... Four outsiders from Harlem and elsewhere in the city have come in and taken over [the schools].

— Albert Shanker[1]

I wish people wouldn't interpret an exclamation of "Drop dead!" as a threat on their lives.

— Reverend C. Herbert Oliver[2]

On September 9, 1968, outside of a junior high school in the northern tip of Manhattan, two lines of students had formed. They were waiting. One group was mostly black; the other was entirely white. The white students were waiting for their escorts. They were going to be taken to a nearby synagogue where a "freedom school" had been organized by striking teachers. The black students were soon to be ushered into their regular public school by teachers who were breaking the strike. One of the nonstriking teachers, outraged at the sight, said to a striking teacher, "This is the most vicious, destructive thing that's ever happened to this school." The striking teacher, unmoved, yelled "Scab!"[3]

Conflicts precipitating this strike had continued through the summer. In the words of Sol Stern, "Paranoia and race hatred seemed thicker than ever in the lingering hot, sticky summer air that smothered the city during all of September. The teachers were on strike again, and Bronx housewives sat in front of their sweltering apartment houses, muttering about the Blacks 'trying to take over.'"[4]

Although many of the original nineteen transferred employees and other union teachers who had in sympathy walked out with them and had since then been voluntarily transferred to other school districts, eighty-three teachers still wished to return to their original assignments in Ocean Hill–Brownsville. The union's present strike was designed to pressure the Board of Education and the mayor to force the local board to rehire these teachers. By the beginning of the 1968 to 1969 school year, however, the experimental district had an almost entirely new staff: The local governing board hired 350 new teachers, more than 50 percent of whom were white and Jewish. Its schools were open and functioning.

The union continued to argue that their concerns were for due process for teachers and the protection of the hard-won rights of job security and tenure, that the Ocean Hill–Brownsville transfers had been both punitive and illegal. Explains Stern, "[The UFT] invoke[d] the ethic of militant trade unionism, civil liberties, and professionalism against what it called the dangers of 'vigilantism' and disruptions of the learning process by politically motivated Black militants."[5] Its members and their supporters claimed that theirs was one of the most progressive unions in the country. They here cited their organized involvement in the freedom schools in Prince Edward County and in Mississippi, their representative contingent in Martin Luther King Jr.'s march for the sanitation workers of Memphis, and their active support for the Poor People's March.

The governing board and the Ocean Hill–Brownsville community maintained that this was a racist strike and that the union was using "guerilla tactics" against the experimental project. In the same way that Jews thirty years before had confronted the resistance of the Irish, who then dominated the school system, the board now resented claims that due process for union teachers required the returning of teachers who were hostile and disruptive to their project when, in the meantime, things had begun to go so well. One white non-striking teacher was reported to have said, "[Union teachers] live in their little worlds, in middle-class enclaves. They automatically see blacks as hostile. They know blacks have suffered and they are afraid they are going to take it out on them. They know they are mediocre, that they're not doing a good job. They think someone is going to find out and get them out."[6]

This sustained gridlock turned Ocean Hill–Brownsville schools into threatening places. Police, working overtime, had been drawn from all over the city. Their barricades were abundant. Picket lines were thick, and the demonstrators were vociferous. When new teachers canvassed students' homes to find out why attendance had been so low, parents frequently told them that they didn't ". . . want to send [their] kids into an armed camp."[7] These fears were well-founded. Children had to squeeze through antagonistic crowds, striking and nonstriking teacher confrontations, and lines of policemen. One parent had been beaten when she insisted that she be allowed to bring her child into the building.[8] Employees were consistently asked for identification and confusion abounded. Charles Isaacs, one of the new teachers, recounted:

At one demonstration, while we were retreating from one line of police advancing in front of us, we turned and found out we were supposed to be retreating from those behind us. The result was blood and chaos. One quiet morning, I myself was arrested because of a similar mixup. One officer said move on; another said stay; whatever I did, I had to end up in jail.[9]

The bitter events, marked by the intervention of the police to preserve "law and order," signaled not only the beginnings of a conflicting relationship between teachers and communities in U.S. society, but also the demise of a particular set of historic coalitions due to an increasingly well-defined distinction between liberal and radical approaches to black emancipatory projects. Literature from the period places an undue emphasis on the changing nature of the relationship between blacks and white Jews.[10] Many historians have described the conflicts in Ocean Hill–Brownsville as a clear marker of the beginning of the end of this relationship. Wrote Jonathan Kaufman, "The Ocean Hill–Brownsville school district in New York was the first place the conflict between Blacks and Jews erupted into open hostility. . . . The sound heard in New York in 1968 and 1969 was the sound of a coalition ripping itself apart. The Ocean Hill–Brownsville clash was the most public sign in the late 1960s that the alliance between blacks and Jews was coming to an end."[11] In a similar vein, Claybourne Carson wrote, "That New York became the setting for this and many subsequent Black–Jewish disputes was also not surprising, for it was there that the group interests of African Americans and Jews were most likely to collide."[12] Paul Buhle and Robin Kelley argued, "Both sides, [blacks and Jews], fought for things progressive activists supported. But both sides fought tenaciously, consequently eliminating the possibility of reconciliation any time soon."[13]

Stated Earl Lewis, "Placed in historical context, therefore, the Ocean Hill–Brownsville controversy symbolized what happened when two group histories converged more than merged.... For those blacks and Jews, ancient prejudices found new meanings as they struggled to maintain or secure their place in American life."[14]

It is difficult to interrogate these claims without a sustained analysis of the role of the UFT in the emergent struggles. I will provide those details in the following chapter. Here, however, I wish to lay out some theoretical background, while introducing some of the union's role, that will illuminate the subsequent discussion. My aim is to explain how Jewish liberalism, as articulated here, framed the politics of Black Power as politically regressive and the work of the governing board as inherently illiberal. Before we turn to the project of disentangling all of the competing interests that set organized blacks and white Jews in an antagonistic relationship, I want to try to explain why a particular mind-set on the part of many of the white Jews sympathetic to the union led to expectations that blacks in Ocean Hill–Brownsville had created a hostile and threatening environment there. Although the perception of such a hostile environment was widespread, suggesting that we must take it seriously, it fails to account for why the new white Jewish employees at the schools had chosen to be in Ocean Hill–Brownsville in the first place, and, once there, why they spoke consistently in defense and support of the project of community control. Rather than dismiss the discrepancy in the attitudes of white Jews involved in the project and those from the outside as one resulting from idiosyncratic personality differences or from a divergent series of encounters with the community, we must see the distinction as rooted in fundamentally opposing positions on the nature of black people and black political progress.

First we must begin by clarifying several definitions. Again, our guiding question is, Why did a particular brand of Jewish liberalism, common among most who opposed the Ocean Hill–Brownsville project, produce a set of formulaic expectations that the governing board and community in District 17 were hostile, threatening and violent, prone to vigilantism and authoritarian control over the free exchange of discourse and ideas?

James Baldwin, writer and public intellectual, was perhaps the best-known critic of white liberalism in the beginnings of the now abundant literature on liberal black-Jewish dialogue. In his 1967 essay, "Negroes are Anti-Semitic Because They're Anti-White," Baldwin argued that, "The root of anti-Semitism among Negroes [was], ironically, the relationship of colored peoples—all over the globe—to the Christian world. . . . In the American context, the most ironical thing about Negro anti-Semitism [was] that the Negro [was] really condemning the Jew for having become an American white man—for having become, in effect, a Christian."[15] Baldwin condemned Jews for the shameless use of the slaughter of six million Jews during the Holocaust as proof of their incapacity for anti-black bigotry.[16] He argued that this claim appeared particularly galling when Jewish landlords demanded outrageous rent from blacks who could not move out of their broken, sagging, rat-infested apartments; when Jewish butchers demanded pay on debts for overpriced meat; when teachers displayed their disdain for black students and school unions collected Baldwin's father's hard-earned money as dues; and when storekeepers established businesses in black neighborhoods, but resided in communities where blacks were prohibited from entering in significant numbers. Baldwin qualifies his description, however, by stating that not all Jews were guilty of such bigotry, and that several of the Jews he encountered were in fact ". . . as thoughtful as the bleak circumstances allowed."[17]

Jewish desires to equate their horrific history with that of American blacks, however, seemed to Baldwin misguided and gratuitous. For Jews, he argued, could be proud, ". . . or at least not ashamed" of their suffering. Theirs had not begun in the United States and could, therefore, become part of a moral history of the Western world. Jews could, unlike blacks, be recognized as contributors to the development of Western heritage and its legacy. Jews could, unlike blacks, rise up against oppression and be called heroes. Indeed, argued Baldwin, "No one [had] ever suggested that the Jew be nonviolent."[18]

In the main, argued Baldwin, Jews and their white counterparts had been overcome by a U.S. identity replete with nostalgia and opportunism. This rendered them incapable of recognizing that the U.S. of which they dreamed and boasted was not the U.S. that blacks saw or inhabited. In this situation, it was not the Jew who could ". . . instruct or console [the Negro]. On the contrary, the American Jew knew just enough about this situation to be unwilling to imagine it again."[19] Indeed, like other white Americans, continued Baldwin, many Jewish Americans witnessing black efforts "to live, not tomorrow, but today," now wanted blacks to wait. Jewish Americans here cited their own experience: "'We suffered, too,' [they say,] 'but we came through, and so will you. In time.'"[20] As they were asked to wait, blacks in Watts and Harlem were being "sentenced to remain there for life."[21] For generations, natives of the Belgian Congo were slaughtered in excess of ten million by Belgians without any indignant Western response.[22] What is more, the framing of the black as "pariah in his own country and as a stranger in the world," combined with systematic ignorance concerning the real violence committed against the black meant that, "when he rose, he was not hailed as a hero fighting for his land, but condemned as a savage, hungry for white flesh."[23] Why must the black's "turn" be *last*?

Baldwin argued that "a genuinely candid confrontation between Negroes and American Jews would certainly prove of inestimable value."[24] It would require as a starting point the recognition that the European serf had created another serf in the New World, this time, Baldwin emphasized, on the basis of color. He claimed that the black could, "if [he was] romantic enough," be disappointed in the Jew for his role in the creation and evasion of this problem. Blaming this record of complicity on his Jewishness, however, seemed senseless and futile to Baldwin. The problem had not, after all, begun with Jews, but instead with ". . . the old, rugged Roman cross."[25]

Through offering a critique of liberal Jewish discourse, Baldwin here helps us to define it. Although he does not describe it as such, he suggests that one of its central components is Jews' quest to describe their historical past (and present encounters with anti-Semitism) as one symmetrical with that of blacks. Baldwin offers that this Jewish project is fundamentally informed by an ahistorical explanation of their own circumstances in America: that everyone comes to the table of contention on equal discursive playing fields under the laws and principles of justice of the society. Although many Jewish liberals admit to social inequalities, they see the space of discourse itself as an equal playing field of interests in which differences can be worked out. In so doing, they have written out the impact that social inequalities have on who gets heard, and they thereby suggest that *what* one argues will have more force than *who* argues. For example, these liberals assume that if blacks were really saying something legitimate, they would be heard. But all of this is premised on the presumption that white America really wants to hear, in a word, *blacks*. As a consequence, Jewish liberals do not recall nor acknowledge their failure to listen to blacks before blacks started taking community action. As a result, they commonly assume that blacks will take violently to the streets as a first rather than a last resort.

Underlying these assumptions is another asserting that good politics is color-blind politics. But advocates of color-blind politics assume that all U.S. citizens have equal access to assimilation.[26] Could blacks (as opposed to some individual black people) in the United States really become non-black?[27] Baldwin would say that the answer is "no" because he argues that serfdom has been recreated in the United States on the basis of race with liberals' complicity—evidenced, for example, by the fact that some of the nation's classic liberal founders were also slave owners and antiblack racists.[28] This means that any attempts on the part of blacks to change this social order short of prolonged discussion and continued "waiting" are deemed inherently illiberal.

We see this phenomenon manifested in responses to the local board's efforts in Ocean Hill–Brownsville. A comparison might prove useful here. Many critics of the Civil Rights movement called it a violent movement. Despite King's formal commitment to nonviolence, the effectiveness of his political struggle lay precisely in the violent responses that his peaceful marches incurred.[29] During these moments in which organized civil rights protests normally culminated, national news broadcasts displayed a picture of segregationist white perversion. Organized white mobs attacked groups of demonstrators whose position seemed undeniably worthy and fundamentally informed by American civic ideals. Organizations of Jewish liberals came out solidly in support of the Civil Rights movement, criticizing charges of its violent nature. As I cited earlier, UFT representatives had been very involved and had continued these efforts back home in localized attempts to integrate New York City's public schools. So why was the violence attributed to Black Power so different? Why did these staunch civil rights activists accept and make these claims themselves in the case of Ocean Hill–Brownsville?

Accusations of violence or of the violent nature of particular activities usually spring from those who feel targeted or attacked by the people or actions so described. When a group of people or a movement is described as violent, as in the case of the Civil Rights movement or the governing board and community in Ocean Hill–Brownsville, this is said, for the most part, by people who feel that this political work and struggle will influence their lives, their property, or their interests in negative ways. In the Civil Rights movement, Jewish liberals worked together with blacks in activities that targeted the state and federal government. The establishment of meaningful civil rights legislation was the central demand. In Ocean Hill–Brownsville and in most black Power struggles, the efforts and goals were localized. They were focused primarily on those who controlled institutions in black communities. This changed the people to be targeted substantively. For in New York City, many institutions in communities of color were owned and run primarily by Jews. This demographic trend was particularly acute in institutions of education—at the elementary, secondary, and college levels. When the local board argued that black civil rights would emerge only through their control over the institutions affecting their communities, liberal Jews, the most common group in the positions of power in New York City schools, immediately became the targets. Unlike during the Civil Rights movement, the actions aimed at them appeared to be violent, hostile, and threatening as a first rather than a last resort. The UFT and their supporters seemed to suggest that power in the hands of a majority Jewish population should not be criticized and fought against.

Let us look more carefully at what was being said about Black Power–guided efforts. One prominent liberal Jewish intellectual working at the New School in the late 1960s described black political struggle on college campuses in the following way:

In America, the student movement has been seriously radicalized whenever police and police brutality intervened in essentially nonviolent demonstrations: occupations of administration buildings, sit-ins, et cetera. Serious violence entered the scene only with the appearance of the Black Power movement on campuses. Negro students, the majority of them admitted without academic qualification, regarded and organized themselves as an interest group, the representatives of the black community. Their interest was to lower academic standards. They were more cautious than the white rebels, but it was clear from the beginning that violence with them was not a matter of theory and rhetoric. Moreover, while the students rebelling in Western countries can nowhere count on popular support outside the universities and as a rule encounter open hostility the moment they use violent means, there stands a large minority of the Negro community behind the verbal or actual violence of the black students. Black violence in America can indeed be understood in analogy to labor violence in America a generation ago; and although ... only Staughton Lynd has drawn the analogy between labor riots and student rebellion explicitly, it seems that the academic establishment, in its curious tendency to yield more to Negro demands, even if they are clearly silly and outrageous, than to disinterested and usually highly moral claims of the white rebels, also thinks in these terms and feels more comfortable when confronted with interests plus violence than when it is a matter of nonviolent "participatory democracy."[30]

Although she was describing efforts made at the level of higher education rather than in public elementary and secondary schools, Hannah Arendt's analysis encapsulates much of what the UFT said about the Ocean Hill–Brownsville project. The local boards in Ocean Hill–Brownsville were believed, in contrast to civil rights activists, to *be* violent: They were seen not only to pose a physical threat to white people, but to seek violently to undercut all established provisions created to ensure quality educational programs and employees. This move was believed by white critics to be driven, not by a solid, if challenging, rationale, but by a poorly conceived and self-aggrandizing quest for power. The travesty, in the minds of the UFT, was that the governing board, led by Rhody McCoy, was being taken seriously by those with the formal powers to enable their project. Furthermore, all of this would come at the cost of historical union efforts to create better working conditions for employees already working in the school system and those still to come. The UFT, though formally in support "of the idea of the experimental project," argued that the actual Ocean Hill–Brownsville project was based on nationalistic and self-interested politics on the part of blacks and romanticization and spinelessness on the part of the mayor and the Board of Education. Why were the latter speaking hopefully of decentralization when its earlier forms had created a school system run by ward bosses and guided by parochialism? The union felt that this ideological turn could only be due to the ways in which it effectively obscured "real concerns" (for example, that the school system required more money).[31] The UFT, like Arendt, took the position that black community leaders were fundamentally self-interested and lacked a sense of civic duty, which rendered them and their work inherently illiberal and violent.

This view was supported by and continues among eminent Jewish intellectuals reflecting on the times. For example, in his 1997 discussion of the conflict in Ocean Hill–Brownsville, Michael Walzer, the influential philosopher and social theorist at the Institute for Advanced Study in Princeton, New Jersey, and former editor of *Dissent*, admitted:

Black Power militancy seemed to me then, and seems to me still, a terrible political mistake. I can understand the need that many Blacks felt to take full charge of their own struggle. Insofar as they did that, they were acting in conformity with the old left maxim: "the liberation of the working class must be the work of the working class." But the workers, after all, were supposed to be the majority of the population when they liberated themselves. American Blacks were and are a minority, with no choice but to engage in coalition politics. That required maintaining links not with "the" Jews but with many Jews and Jewish organizations and also with people in the union and the white churches and with feminists and even with urban white ethnics inside the Democratic Party. To try to fight alone, without any of these allies, meant to fight with no hope of success. Black Power was mostly a politics of gesture— and when it brought no quick victories, the gestures turned nasty.

I want to distinguish carefully between gestures and interests. The two divided Blacks and Jews at roughly the same time, but not in the same way or with the same effects. Crudely put, the divergent interests could have been negotiated and compromised, case by case, were it not for the often threatening symbolism of the gestures.[32]

In concert with Arendt, Walzer offers a psychological explanation of black militancy, suggesting that it was driven by emotional need rather than by political insight and understanding. He argues that this mode of political activity is seductive but corrosive. It moves black energies away from efforts to form powerful and necessary coalitions and in so doing makes liberal negotiation impossible.

While raising questions about the extent to which the governing board was really working with its community, UFT accounts of Ocean Hill–Brownsville never distinguished between comments made by the local board's formal representatives and by random others. The writings about the community produced by the union are thus replete with "Black Power gestures" often taken from angry confrontations in the midst of ongoing strikes. We might wonder how the UFT would have looked if its formal position on the experiment and decentralization had been formulated on the basis of striking teachers' angry comments alone. The conflict might have then stood squarely as one between dissenters of decentralization and advocates of community control. Instead, it was black anger that was seen as ultimately transcending the particularities of a black community project, which set the stage for a conflict between antagonists of community control and racism on the one hand and a group of anti-Jewish racists on the other. In their attacks, the union, furthermore, portrayed the leadership in District 17 as a group of power-hungry individuals, which created the addendum of anti-Jewish opportunists.

The representation of the community as single-mindedly black because of the Black Power advocacy of some of their leadership was a gross mischaracterization. The Black Power movement, as a nationwide movement, had brought many blacks, Puerto Ricans, Dominicans, Native Americans, and Asian Americans together.[33] These groups often shared neighborhoods faced with similar problems. The governing board was itself comprised of blacks, Puerto Ricans, and whites, and it was heavily supported by most of its new white and Jewish employees and by leaders of the Community Studies Program at Queens College. Likewise, many teachers and community leaders in other parts of the city championed their efforts, supporting their attempts to keep the eight schools in the area open during UFT strikes and writing extensive articles refuting the negative ways in which individual members of the school community and their work was represented. This reality was obscured in most UFT writings as it is in the long excerpt from Walzer above. This distortion is due in part to the ways in which liberal conceptions of conflict fail to leave room for the role of power and political accessibility. They saw *Black* Power as excluding *Colored* Power, which could be translated as *Disadvantaged Community's* Power. Why should the achievement of Jewish Power in New York City be treated as more inclusive than the struggle for Black Power, when it was clear that the practice of colored exclusion remained under white Jewish rule as it did under other white ethnic groups that preceded them?

The attack on Black Power collapsed into the characterization of the board and its supporters as violent and anti-Semitic. The efforts of the governing board to dispel these charges were to no avail. When a set of explicitly anti-Semitic pamphlets mysteriously emerged, the UFT reproduced and disseminated them throughout the city. Earl Lewis and Charles Isaacs have protested that the documents had not been produced by a local organization, as the union claimed, and despite suspicions that they had instead been written by a few non-affiliated individuals, by the Federal Bureau of Investigation's Covert Intelligence Program (COINTELPRO) employees, or the union itself, the union and its supporters claimed that the content was truly representative of what was going on in Ocean Hill–Brownsville schools.[34] My goal here is not to discredit the legitimacy of the angered Jewish response to anti-Semitic writings. Rather it is to uncover and make sense of the discrepancy between the local board's statement on anti-Semitism, the content of the pamphlets, and what the UFT insisted was "the view" advocated by teachers and administrators of the Ocean Hill–Brownsville schools.

On November 11, 1968, the *New York Times* published an advertisement, "Anti- Semitism?—A Statement by the Teachers of Ocean Hill–Brownsville to the People of New York," written and submitted by a group of recently hired Ocean Hill–Brownsville teachers. It said:

> We state unequivocally that by their words and actions [the local board and Ocean Hill–Brownsville administrators] have shown that they will not tolerate any form of anti-Semitism. Furthermore, we resent the continued allegations that are being made against the governing board when we know that they are untrue. Here are the words of the Ocean Hill-Brownsville governing board on this matter:
>
> "The Ocean Hill–Brownsville governing board, as well as the entire Ocean Hill–Brownsville demonstration district, has never tolerated nor will it ever tolerate anti-Semitism in any form. Anti-Semitism has no place in our hearts or minds and indeed never in our schools.
>
> "While certain anti-Semitic literature may have been distributed outside our school buildings, there is absolutely no connection between these acts and the thought and intents of the Ocean Hill–Brownsville governing board. We disclaim any responsibility for this literature and have in every way sought to find its source and take appropriate action to stop it."

The authors concluded:

> The acts of the board, however, are more important than their words. When the governing board recruited 350 new teachers last summer, more than 50 percent of them were Jewish. Are these anti-Semitic actions?

It is interesting to note that without the teachers' republication of the local board's statement against anti-Semitism, it was unlikely for it to have been heard. Although reiterated by McCoy in a public interview, the local board's pronouncement was not widely reported. Even though the November 11 statement by teachers invoked some response, it was still rather limited in comparison to the press given to Jewish outrage over the content of the pamphlets. Perhaps the most often repeated section of these was the following:

> If African American History and Culture is to be taught to our Black Children it Must Be Done by African-Americans Who Identify With and Who Understand the Problem. It is Impossible for the Middle East Murderers of Colored People to Possibly Bring to This Important Task the Insight, The Concern, The Exposing of the Truth That is a Must If The Years of Brainwashing and Self-Hatred That Has Been Taught To Our Black Children By These Bloodsucking Exploiters and Murderers Is to Be Overcome . . . Get out, Stay Out, Staff Off, Shut Up, Get Off Our Backs, Or Your Relatives In The Middle East Will Find Themselves Giving Benefits To Raise Money To Help You Get Out From Under The Terrible Weight Of An Enraged Black Community.[35]

It is implausible that a group of sophisticated school leaders and experienced activists would express their views in such a way, especially given their aims to work with the predominantly Jewish Board of Education. Although Black Power advocates had offered strong criticisms of the nation of Israel and its policies in relation to Palestinians, it should be borne in mind that anti-Zionism and anti-Semitism are not identical. Many liberal Jews, however, saw the two as equivalent. In a similar way, this writing clearly contradicts what the local board had said about and done in terms of hiring practices. McCoy had offered a more nuanced description of what black-controlled schooling meant. While highly critical of the white "stranglehold" on black communities, he had never suggested that some whites (or Jews) were incapable of being allies in and to the experimental district. In "An Open Letter to Michael Harrington," Dwight Mac-Donald wrote:

> Anyone who has heard, on television or in private meetings, Mr. McCoy, the [Reverend] Oliver, or some of the principals of the district, as I have, knows they are serious educators and that support from such fantasts [*sic*] is as welcome to them as an endorsement by the Black Panthers would be to [conservative] Senator Brooke of Massachusetts.[36]

One Jewish teacher in Ocean Hill-Brownsville, Charles Isaacs, states that he had never seen any "hate" literature in his school besides that distributed by the UFT. He suggested that the union had in fact used the contrived issue of anti-Semitism to exploit the real fears of the liberal Jewish community. He wrote:

> [T]he community and the governing board have demonstrated again and again that these fears [of anti-Semitism] are unfounded. On the day before Rosh Hashanah, the governing board distributed to all the children in our schools a leaflet explaining the holiday, what it means to Jewish people, and why all the city schools are closed on that day. As far as I know, no other school district has taken the trouble to do this.[37]

Anti-Semitism in this context had become so wedded to anti-liberalism, that all efforts at rational argument proved futile. Perhaps this point will become clearer when we consider a second pamphlet (to follow). Although it had no explicitly anti-Semitic content, it was redistributed by the UFT with the others that did.

The UFT advertised this piece as a direct transcription of an eighth-grade social studies class taught by Leslie Campbell. Campbell, along with McCoy, Herman Ferguson, and Reverend Oliver, had been singled out by the UFT and the press sympathetic to it, as the most militant and power-hungry members of the governing board. It was thought that although in the minority, they had been the ones to advocate and push for a Black Power takeover of the schools. One union librarian said, "I helped start the experimental district. We wouldn't have any trouble if all those militants, the Sonny Carsons, the Fergusons, the Ralph Poynters, the Leslie Campbells, hadn't taken over. Leslie Campbell teaches his kids not to steal from each other; he tells them to get a piece, to go get ready for the war."[38] Charles Isaacs, who was not in the union, offered a quite different description of Campbell, as an innovative teacher doing innovative work. He wrote:

> When I first met Campbell, I hardly knew what to expect: physically, vocally, and intellectually, he seemed far larger than the norm, and supposedly, he had no use for whites. Two months of conversation and observation have discredited the latter speculation and confirmed the former. Campbell wants to see the institutions that dominate the lives of black people controlled by those people, not by white colonial masters, but he recognizes the role that can be played by white allies in the struggle.[39]

Although we will be discussing the class "transcription" as disseminated by the UFT, it is important to note that *Education News*, the magazine from which it was taken, subsequently sued the union for composing and distributing the reprint in a misleading way. What is more, the lesson is presented as having occurred in a school that was never part of the Ocean Hill–Brownsville district.[40] Nonetheless the complete pamphlet read as follows:

> "What Black Power Teaches":
> During the New York City teachers' strike, . . . a reporter [from] *Education News* visited the eighth-grade class taught by Leslie J. Campbell, a leader of the African-American Teachers Association.
>
> . . . These are excerpts from [his] account of the class session.
>
> Mr. Campbell: Now, class, ask Timmy questions about our Afro-American heritage and Black Power.
> Pupil 1: We have leaders like Martin Luther King, and he tells us to be peaceful, and then we have leaders like Malcolm X and Rap Brown and they tell us to use violence. Who is right?
> Mr. Campbell: Timmy, tell him what you learned?
> Timmy: Well, I think Martin Luther King is not so good. Whitey don't want to give us anything, so we got to fight for it.
> Pupil 2: Why do we have to fight? Why can't we just demonstrate peacefully like Dr. King?
> Mr. Campbell: Whitey doesn't listen. The only thing he understands is when we get up and start throwing bricks and Molotov cocktails.
> Pupil 3: What is Black Power?
> Mr. Campbell (writing on the blackboard): Black Power is control by Afro-Americans of three things. The first

is political power, the second is economic power, the
third part is social. We have 12 per cent of the people.
There are 100 senators. How many are black? One,
and he [Edward Brooke, R. of Mass.] is an Uncle Tom.
Now, Timmy, would you like an Afro-American state?
Timmy: Well, I don't know. Sometimes I do and some-
times I don't.
Mr. Campbell: Think! Our own state for black people.
Timmy: Yeah, I guess that would be good.

It is Time For Citizens To Know The Truth! Leslie
Campbell is still on the staff at JHS 271, "instructing"
and "organizing." Write to Mayor Lindsay today.
Demand an end to all racism in our schools.[41]

This detailed a description of a class requires an extended visit
and careful observation. That a reporter from *Education News*
undertook such a visit is a rarer occurrence than some might
think. It might be useful to note that very few teachers ever
visit their colleagues' classes in this sustained way. Administrators at most schools do so only when they are formally evaluating their staff. Indeed, many educational leaders committed to
the reinvigoration of pre-service and in-service teacher training have advocated for their indispensable need for classrooms
to have an open-, rather than closed-, door policy.

Such a detailed description of any teacher's class requires
the kind of visitation and observation that a reporter from
Education News here undertook. It might be useful to note that
very few teachers ever visit their colleagues' classes in this
sustained a way. Administrators do so only when they are formally evaluating their staff. Given the controversy surrounding Campbell, curiosity to see him in action may seem
unsurprising. But my point is rather different: Accounts of
what other teachers were doing in their daily classes might
have been equally alarming, if for different reasons. The
charge of "organizing" leveled against Campbell has a long

history. Unless we assume that dissenting ideas disappear over time, which I do not, we would probably encounter more of them if we looked. Communists, liberals, and conservatives have all received this charge, especially where they have represented a minority opinion in their schools. Likewise, one might raise questions about the extent to which one can describe a teacher's project with his or her students based on one brief exchange. After all, teachers are, for the most part, in contact with their students five days a week for most of the year. Although the duration gives them ample time to communicate their beliefs to their students, the nuances of what they find important to teach manifests in all the subtle interchanges that occur between instructors and their students over time. I say none of this to suggest that Mr. Campbell did not strongly advocate for the necessity of Black Power and its usefulness to young black students. That point is evident regardless of the specific difference between his actual class and the one represented in the pamphlet. Rather, I argue instead that the concerns raised by *Education News* over this reprint and the popularity of Campbell among new white teachers suggest that his understanding of these issues and his commitment to their transmission was more subtle than the preceding document conveyed. Addressing Black Power may have been an appropriate historic issue to discuss, especially for a neighborhood besieged by controversy over its role in the community. Could one imagine studying the 1960s today without a discussion of Black Power?

Many educators have offered descriptive accounts of how the mood of the 1960s permeated the teaching atmosphere. Teachers drawn to the profession by a belief in the need for dramatic social change felt that these transformations would soon be under way. Their job was to prepare their students to be the inheritors of the soon-to-be changed political order. In retrospect, this goal may seem naïve. However, based on teachers' reports, the stirrings of social action might be evidenced in those rare instances when young people demonstrated a lively interest in learning about the past. This is especially significant in an otherwise present-centered society where high school students consistently rank history as one of their least favorite subjects. Some critics might argue that this appeal of history might stem from its vast oversimplification on the part of dogmatic teachers, suggesting that students' increased interest was a result of a drop in the level of rigor of course material. Does it not make sense, however, to be more interested in something that one feels to be immediately relevant? Education studies that have sought to answer this question offer a clear and resounding, "yes."

Given this, and the nature of the experiment in Ocean Hill–Brownsville, it might seem obvious that a teacher working with a predominantly black class of students would talk about Martin Luther King Jr. and Malcolm X. Critics of the schools they attended were, after all, advocating one position over the other. "Who is right?" is an excellent hermeneutic question to pose to middle-school students. It offers broad implications; black communities—including Ocean Hill–Brownsville—historians, and activists still see it as a question that provokes meaningful, albeit heated, debate.

Of course many critics discount all this, arguing that when considering questions of violence with young people, one should not suggest any air of moral ambiguity. Some believe that the issue of violence as a method of social action should not be open to debate. Young people, it is generally argued, cannot and should not attempt to distinguish between different kinds or uses of violence. Social critics state that public school children already manifest too many violent tendencies. These pedagogical mantras are intensified in schools in inner city communities. It is assumed that anything less than a blanket statement against violence—for example, you will be expelled if you initiate a physical fight—will create a bloody domino effect. While desires to ebb the flow of youth violence seem unquestionably laudatory, one would think that if any young people were to understand the subtle distinctions between different kinds of violence, then it would surely be the kind of young people Campbell taught.

I interpret Campbell's claim that "whitey" would not listen to black social activists without recourse to violent measures, as meaning that whites would not be willing to cede power unless some type of organized and politically threatening black political pressure existed. Recall Frederick Douglass's famous encomium: "Power concedes nothing without demand. It never did and it never will."[42]

I do not think that Campbell was using the word "listen" as an invitation to whites in power to engage in liberal discourse. Unfortunately, both the Civil Rights movement and the conflict surrounding the students' school seemed to prove this claim. As blacks organized for control, support for reform of ghetto schools through direct black involvement decreased substantially. The threats that many people believed that the Ocean Hill–Brownsville community posed, however, did lead to more immediate response from the mayor than earlier efforts had produced. Such responses increased the relevance of Black Power as a topic for classroom discussions.

Campbell's description of the three dimensions of power and of the one black senator might, arguably, be viewed as overly simplistic. For eighth graders, however, the analysis represented highly complex and rigorous subject for course discussion. Campbell's request that his students imagine a nation for black diasporic people was intended to help them to develop their conceptual abilities by addressing what he believed should and would engage them. When U.S. high school students study the Revolutionary era one would hope that similar kinds of questions are raised. Isn't this, after all, the kind of imaginative work required in all good historical investigation?

The pamphlet, excerpted from a longer piece in *Education News*, unsurprisingly failed to mention that Campbell was one teacher in a staff that was 70 percent white. The majority of this group of teachers had supported the institutionalizing of an Afro-American core course of Campbell's design. How this lesson fit into the larger project was not outlined in the pamphlet, however. Pictured, instead, is a black teacher encouraging "gesturing," as Walzer might put it, rather than genuine engagement with his students over political ideas.

This depiction of Campbell's class rendered him persona non grata. The UFT filed a formal complaint against him and his appropriateness as a teacher with the Board of Education. Campbell's reputation was worsened by his appearance on Julius Lester's WBAI radio show *The Great Proletarian Cultural Revolution*.[43] Lester, in the spirit of liberal dialogue, had arranged for Campbell to help him lead a discussion about black anti-Semitism on the air. Lester, who visited J.H.S. 271, the Ocean Hill–Brownsville school in which Campbell worked, was surprised to find that the majority of teachers at the school were Jewish. "They [were]," reflected Lester, "frustrated and angry that their story [was] not being heard." His taped interviews with them "[had] no effect, of course." When Lester visited Campbell's class, he found himself "impressed by his gentleness as well as his effectiveness as a history teacher."[44] On the night of the show, Lester asked Campbell to read a few of the poems that one of his students had written. One was an anti-Semitic poem. Campbell initially refused, suggesting that Lester must have been crazy and clearly had no idea what the consequences would be. Lester insisted. He argued that it was necessary for liberal Jews to take seriously the fact that the continued conflict and strikes in their community were inspiring anger in black schoolchildren. Finally, Campbell agreed. The poem was dedicated to Albert Shanker. It read:

Hey, Jew boy, with that yarmulke on your head
You pale-faced Jew boy—I wish you were dead.
I can see you Jew boy—no you can't hide.
I got a scoop on you—yeh, you gonna die.
I'm sick of your stuff
Every time I turn 'round—you pushin' my ear into the ground
I'm sick of hearing about your suffering in Germany
I'm sick about your escape from tyranny;
I'm sick of seeing in everything you do
About the murder of six million Jews
Hitler's reign lasted for only fifteen years
For that period of time you shed crocodile tears
My suffering lasted for over 400 years, Jew boy,
And the white man only let me play with his toys
Jew boy, you took my religion and adopted it for you
But you know that Black people were the original Hebrews
When the U.N. made Israel a free independent State
Little four- and five-year-old boys threw hand grenades
They hated the Black Arabs with all their might
And you, Jew boy, said it was all right
Then you came to America, land of the free
And took over the school system to perpetrate white
supremacy
Guess you know, Jew boy, there's only one reason you made it
You had a clean white face, colorless, and faded
I hated you Jew boy, because your hangup was the Torah
And my only hangup was my color.[45]

A discussion with listeners followed. One caller asked why Lester had Campbell read it. Lester explained again: It was an ugly poem but it was not nearly as ugly as what had been going on around the schools; he knew half of WBAI's subscribers would immediately cancel their subscriptions to the station, but he also knew it was necessary to clear the air of hysteria and turn to the real issue, whether whites could discuss giving black communities the power that they possessed. Lester, pleased by the discussion that emerged, recorded the show and replayed it over the course of the following two days. A few weeks later, the UFT filed a complaint with the Federal Communications Commission against WBAI.

Although WBAI's general manager Frank Millspaugh and program director Dale Minor presented a special half-hour program in which they "supported the station's right to air such things," the *New York Times* carried a front-page headline about the poem and the UFT complaint. The *Times* quoted Shanker and did not contact Lester then or ever. Despite his denials of anti-Semitism in a *New York Post* article, Lester was branded an anti-Semite in Jewish papers across the nation.[46] None of these publications sent representatives to try to contact him. A leaflet circulated by the Jewish Defense League (JDL), who was campaigning to have Lester fired, depicted him with a swastika and a young woman wearing a fur jacket, fur boots, and carrying a picket sign that read, "Do not use Jews for scapegoats." At the bottom it read, "Cancel out Julius or he may cancel out you!"[47]

A week later, two students from Ocean Hill–Brownsville were on Lester's show. During the course of the interview, one of them, Tyrone Woods, said Hitler should have made more Jews into lampshades. "I want[ed] to kill him!" said Lester, feeling that his adolescent display would be taken for more than it was.

The *New York Times* "dutifully reported" Woods's remark.[48] The JDL organized a demonstration outside the station for the following week. They were going to demand that Lester be fired and that his station license be revoked. Wrote Lester:

Naively, I thought that airing the poem would facilitate contact between Jews and blacks. Jews needed to know how damaging Shanker's remarks had been; they needed to know the depth of black anger over the UFT's opposition to community control and how they were being exploited by the false accusation of black anti-Semitism. They needed to know that if they wanted blacks to care about Jewish suffering, they had to care about black suffering. As crude and obscene as the poem was, I heard in it an excruciating paroxysm of pain. It was pain expressed as anger at Jews, many of whom found identity by borrowing suffering from the Holocaust while remaining blithely blind to the suffering of black people around them and actively opposing the political means blacks used to alleviate a portion of that suffering.[49]

WBAI stood solidly behind Lester, refusing the demands of the JDL. Lester, however, soon left New York and the station. In a private interview, he confessed that the conflict in Ocean Hill–Brownsville had been so upsetting that he no longer wished to speak of it. He had said all that he had to say about it on the air at the time. Although open dialogue had seemed desirable and possible for a brief period, his attempts to sustain it had been effectively undercut. While the UFT and liberal Jews generally argued that blacks needed to pursue racial justice through liberal democratic measures, black efforts to do so were deemed irremediably illiberal.

4

When Some Workers Don't Look Toward the Left

The Battle with the United Federation of Teachers

The fight for Ocean Hill–Brownsville was the correct kind of fight for the Old Left. For the teachers' strike was not, as some people claimed, race warfare—it was class warfare. A middle class traditionally arises out of commerce and trade. But in America, a new phenomenon had come into being: the laboring middle class. If a man works in a Pittsburgh steel mill and owns a home, two cars, and a pleasure boat, then he is a member of the middle class regardless of what he does to earn his salary. And if he spends his time in fear that the underclass will take away what he's gotten, then his attitudes are as middle-class as his possessions. The trade union movement has been wildly successful. The only members of the lower classes, in American today, are the unemployed and the ununionized—which means, essentially, the nonwhites. In short, Old Left has become New Right.[1]

—Robert Rossner

The New York City teacher is a member of an aspiring economic class first, and a teacher second.... Most important of all, in regard to the present struggle of black and Puerto Rican people for "local control," he does not feel that he is the singular perpetrator of education crimes committed against black and Puerto Rican children, and he therefore does not feel that he should be made the scapegoat to assuage the guilt felt by much more affluent whites over their much larger role in committing these crimes.[2]

—Patrick Harnett

Paul Buhle and Robin Kelley wrote of the conflict in Ocean Hill–Brownsville:

The fight between Black and Puerto Rican community activists and the predominantly Jewish UFT irrevocably damaged the liberal Black-Jewish alliance. Old Left Jewish radicals who had cultivated links with working-class Black and Latino communities were suddenly forced to choose between supporting a labor conflict and an important community issue affecting aggrieved populations of color. Both sides fought for things progressive activists supported. But both sides fought tenaciously, consequently eliminating the possibility of reconciliation any time soon.[3]

Why did such a forced choice emerge for both sides? Why were these two groups not the most obvious of allies? Did they need to become enemies? Did the protection of working teachers require fighting the Ocean Hill– Brownsville community? Was the fight for community control inherently anti-labor? What role did anti-Semitism and anti-black racism play in configuring "the two sides"? Can a new understanding of the role of liberalism help us make sense of the demise of this alliance? Unless we are willing to support the position that the majority of black teachers and new white employees of the local board were duped by leaders of an inherently flawed community project, we must take seriously why, in the midst of this struggle, they split so categorically with the union. It is not my goal to chastize the union. Rather, it is to understand why a union that identified itself as "progressive," led the crusade against community control in Ocean Hill– Brownsville. For although their request required the consent of the Board of Education and Mayor John Lindsay, it was the union that negotiated the suspension of the experimental board and the dismantling of the demonstration project. I will argue that the union, although working to protect the class interest of their constituency, defined these goals in such a way that made solidarity with the black (and Puerto Rican) community impossible. Let us begin by laying out what was at stake for "the two sides" to which Buhle and Kelly referred.

Recall that in the aftermath of failed efforts to integrate New York City public schools, some members of the poor black and Latino communities pushed for control of their local schools. They wanted to rid their schools of racism, which they believed was perpetrated primarily through the control of their schools by outsiders. Mayor John Lindsay and the Board of Education, together with a grant from the Ford Foundation, responded to these demands by creating three experimental districts. One of these was District 17 in Ocean Hill– Brownsville. The precise outline of the local board's powers in this area was never agreed upon. Ironically, they were clearly defined only when the Board of Education attempted to take apart and replace the experiment's administrative staff. The local community board itself had taken some time to figure out what their demands for community control required in terms of practical administrative powers. This is perhaps less surprising when we note that many of the local administrators had never done this kind of work before. Some had been principals or assistant principals or leaders of churches, poverty agencies, or grass-roots organizations. Their lack of formal professional experience did not concern them. They felt, in fact, that the requirements for the job of running school districts were part of the problem: Through the invocation of "professional standards," few representatives of communities like their own filled such positions. What is more, proceduralism and the various credentialing processes had not ensured that people hired for these posts were able to perform the duties entailed of them. They soon found that in addition to control over their own budget and curriculum, they would need authority over their staff. This entailed the power to hire, fire, and transfer their employees as they deemed necessary. There had to be a way to ensure appropriate staff without violating teachers' rights.

Jonathan Kaufman has noted that in 1954, a few weeks after the Supreme Court outlawed school segregation, Kenneth Clark, the NAACP Legal Defense Fund's star witness, had charged that the segregation of New York's schools had resulted in a disproportionate number of all-black schools with fewer experienced teachers than in other districts.[4] No systematic changes had been made to address the situation he described. In 1968, many of the communities' deepest concerns and sharpest criticisms were about teachers at their local schools. The governing board needed to take these points seriously. Despite their innovation, they had inherited from former district administrators the staff of teachers with whom Ocean Hill–Brownsville parents were discontent. While the governing board made careful distinctions between sympathetic, effective teachers on the one hand and antipathetic and ineffective teachers on the other, the majority of teachers were fearful of the dramatic and quick transformation of their workplaces. They noted with alarm the local board's criticisms of professional standards and rules. Unclear as to what their new administrators' goals really were, many turned to their local UFT chapters for clarification.

This move angered and frustrated the governing board, which was trying to establish its legitimacy while attempting to change the nature of some of the professional standards for which the union had long struggled. While Rhody McCoy and his staff attempted to ensure job security for their new employees who were not protected by the regular district measures, they were being criticized for trying to evade protectorate measures won by the UFT. Likewise, while the local board attempted to create employment opportunities for their own community through paraprofessional programs, positions for people who would function as liaisons between the community and the school, and other such projects, their efforts were being undermined by the union, who claimed that the board was using decentralization and community control as means of undercutting the labor cause in New York City. It was clear to the local board then, that when the UFT spoke of "labor," they were not referring to poor communities of color like their own.

The local board also offered its own formal criticisms of the union, suggesting that in its primary focus on politics and economics, they did not take into account the existential dimensions of black poverty.[5] Sol Stern, one critic of the UFT's activity, said this:

> White, centrally controlled schools mean in effect no learning but an atmosphere of fear and alienation for teacher and child alike. Community-controlled schools, as anyone who visited Ocean Hill–Brownsville must know, at least provide an atmosphere of warmth and dignity. I asked two fifteen-year-old girls who had graduated from JHS 271 last year, and who thus had lived through that school's agonizing transition from white to black control, what the difference was between the two principals. One of them said, "Well, Mr. Bloomfield [whom the UFT and Board of Education wished to have as unit administrator] used to hide in his office all day—

whenever there was trouble he would send one of his assistant principals to check it out. He was like a scared mouse. Mr. Harris we could always see. And when he took over he asked all the classes to elect a delegate to come and meet with him and tell him what our complaints were."[6]

Although McCoy might have emphasized that the school atmosphere significantly impacted the quality of student learning and therefore contended with the idea that "at least" the district was hospitable, a community like the one cultivated by Mr. Harris was precisely what the local board had been advocating for. Schools did not have to be horrific places replete with teachers antagonistic toward black students. There were, argued McCoy, some who actually preferred to work with Ocean Hill–Brownsville students, who performed extraordinarily well at the task. Just as clear signs of progress were emerging and there was enough stability to allow administrators to turn to questions of the school's educational programs, the governing board believed that the UFT had come in to sabotage the local board's efforts. Why did the interests of the union's constituency—in the main, lower-middle-class white teachers—have to be at odds with those of the people in Ocean Hill–Brownsville?

McCoy's transfer of nineteen staff members to central headquarters was hotly disputed. While the UFT claimed that the local board had violated due process procedures, the New York Civil Liberties Union jumped to McCoy's defense, underwriting a press release by the organization's associate director, Ira Glasser. He wrote:

At first—and this appears to be a fact that is not generally known—McCoy tried to reassign the nineteen *within* the experimental district. According to the Niemeyer Report,

McCoy had the authority to do that based on oral information he had received. Yet when some teachers refused
to be transferred, the Board of Education refused to back
up McCoy's authority. Apparently it was clearly within
McCoy's authority to transfer personnel *within* his district
until he actually tried to exercise it.[7]

Glasser added that when McCoy had then asked to transfer the nineteen to another district, Superintendent Donovan
denied the request. The local board was forced to send notices
to the group of employees, referring them to Board of Education headquarters for reassignment. "This transfer was interpreted by the professional staff, the community at large, and
the press as a dismissal," said Glasser. He wrote in the local
board's defense:

> Dismissals must be accompanied by the requirements of
> due process, including written notice of charges, right to
> a hearing, right to confront witnesses, right to call wit-
> nesses, right to introduce evidence, right to receive tran-
> script, right to appeal, etc. The bylaws mandate these
> requirements for regular teachers, and the UFT contract
> extends the requirements to substitute teachers. But nei-
> ther the bylaws nor the contract mandate the require-
> ments of due process for mere transfers. Article II,
> section 101.1 of the bylaws says: "Transfers of members
> of the teaching and supervising staff from one school to
> another shall be made by the superintendent of schools,
> who shall report immediately such transfer to the Board
> of Education for its consideration and action."[8]

The purpose of these provisions, argued Glasser, was to
allow the superintendent maximum flexibility to transfer
teachers. They also illustrated that teachers' job rights did not

include the right to choose their own assignments. Many hundreds of such transfers took place each year without objection or even note. Despite this, the UFT demanded a due process hearing. Glasser noted that at the same time as these demands were being made, the UFT had sent representatives to Albany to lobby against community control. "It certainly seem[ed] abundantly clear," he concluded, "that the due process issue as used by the UFT was nothing but a smokescreen behind which the effort to discredit and destroy community control could go on."[9] The union never admitted that it had made special allowances for teachers to transfer out of the experimental district whenever they wished to do so. Under normal conditions, teachers are required to remain in a school in which they are placed for a minimum of five years before requesting a transfer.[10]

Despite all the questions raised about the UFT's actions, the governing board was called to present and defend their claims against the transferred nineteen in court. Not forewarned about such a move, the governing board's lawyers came in unprepared—without the evidence and witnesses necessary to defend their actions effectively. The board's case against the teachers was dismissed. The Board of Education demanded the return of these teachers and their union supporters who had also been replaced over the summer. When the local board refused, the UFT went on strike. These strikes continued, on and off, until the experimental district was finally disbanded at the end of 1969 through a new decentralization law that absorbed the eight experimental schools of District 17 into Brooklyn's District 23. In each strike, charges of anti-Semitism escalated. The response the UFT demanded of the Board of Education was the immediate suspension of McCoy and his administrative staff and the closing of a school in which UFT teachers felt they had been harassed. The Board complied with the first demand twice and once with the second. One teacher wrote, "This issue of anti-Semitism preys on the fears of one ethnic group that united behind us can destroy us."[11]

When the UFT printed 500,000 copies of a series of photocopied anti-Semitic pamphlets as examples of the board's views, of "what [it] was up against," the local board grew outraged.[12] Numerous community efforts to denounce their content proved fruitless. The governing board could not shake the public opinion that they were nationalistic and Jew-hating. Each charge gave fuel to the union's efforts to fight those who should have been its constituency. Jonathan Kaufmann saw charges of anti-Semitism as little more than a labor strategy. He wrote:

> As a device to win the strike, Shanker's decision to print the handouts was a brilliant tactical move. Overnight it changed the debate from one over community control and decentralization—over which many in the city, including Jews, were divided—into a debate over anti-Semitism in the Black community. Are these the kinds of things, Shanker asked, that you want said in your schools? Are these the kind of people you want running the schools and teaching children? Many Jews were already unhappy with the rising militancy and anti-white sentiment emanating from the more militant parts of the civil rights movement. Most Jews in New York still considered themselves liberals, but many, especially in working-class neighborhoods, were becoming scared.[13]

This UFT move changed the tenor of debate over the schools dramatically. Indeed to this day, many historians and residents in New York City at the time recall the event as representative of the deteriorating relations between blacks and Jews more than they do as a conflict over schooling. Why had the UFT blamed a poor community of color for anti-Semitism when these comments were made by individuals struggling at the hands of a white establishment that was predominantly Jewish? Did they really believe that anti-Semitism was being taught in Ocean Hill–Brownsville?

The UFT, though ostensibly internally divided over the concept of decentralization, had many concerns about the actual proposals and demands that experimental district leaders had begun to circulate. Combined with growing talk of community control, members of the UFT feared a return to a school system reminiscent of earlier years, when school arrangements made efforts to protect teachers' rights very difficult. They felt that only cynicism could seduce New York City leaders to think nostalgically of the old neighborhood schools that were once controlled by local ward bosses and wrought with interethnic conflict. They wondered why New York City leaders would advocate for parochialism or, in this case, black nationalism.

The centralizing and standardizing of the public schools had, after all, led to the professionalization of school administrators and staff, and in so doing had created the space for unions to protect the school system's employees. "Those who fought for the establishment of teachers' unions were then considered radicals and civil rights activists."[14] Supporters acknowledged the union "not only as a force for winning rights for teachers but as a progressive, liberalizing force in a stagnant trade union movement."[15] Only a few years earlier, the most socially conscious New York City teachers were the ones who fought the union battles. "The first teachers' strike in 1960 brought out only 7,500 teachers to walk the picket lines and jeopardize their jobs."[16] Those most concerned about job security were the ones who crossed the picket lines.[17]

Although the UFT had no special love for the Board of Education, *the* centralized power in the school system, union leaders felt that Board members were at least recognizable targets in their attempts to expand teachers' rights. Their ideas about organizing activities and their political aspirations had been profoundly influenced by welfare-state socialism of the 1930s and 1940s. The UFT believed that substantive measures to further social justice could only come from centralized bodies or the federal level. They cited New Deal efforts as an example of what centralized power could mandate. When left to smaller communities, they felt, actions could only represent localized, narrow, and self-aggrandizing interests. Localized efforts supposedly would never lead to integrative or redistributive measures. In an anecdote documented by Dwight MacDonald, Michael Harrington supposedly said of Shanker, "There'll be real problems for him if the school system is split into thirty or forty or sixty autonomous districts. . . . Well . . . even thirty seems too many . . . fragmentation . . . chaos . . . and those white racists on Staten Island could fire all the liberal and colored teachers."[18]

These positions are clearly evidenced in the political affiliations of union leaders. Wrote Sol Stern:

> An interlocking directorate between the teachers union and various New York social democratic organizations could easily be charted. Union President Albert Shanker was himself once a member of the Young People's Socialist League and [was in 1968] a member of the board of the League for Industrial Democracy (LID), a socialist education organization. Charles Cogen, who had preceded Shanker as UFT president and groomed him for the job, was once Socialist Party candidate for the City Council. One of Shanker's two executive assistants, Sandra Feldman, [was] wife to Paul Feldman, editor of the Socialist Party organ *New America*. Shanker's administrative assistant [was] the wife of Max Shachtman, a mentor of

[Michael] Harrington and [Bayard] Rustin and the chief ideologue of the more esoteric of old left sects. Rustin, Harrington, Paul Feldman, and Tom Kahn, the executive director of the LID, are all personally close to Shanker and serve as a kind of "kitchen cabinet" for his union.[19]

Stern concluded that this list included most of the ranks of the conservative socialist movement in the U.S. at the time. All of these groups had argued that race was not intrinsic to issues of class inequality—the category through which they deemed the struggle for social change should take place in the United States.

I am not suggesting that all of these connections add up to some sort of subversive, conspiratorial activity.[20] Rather, such an outline helps us to explain why, during the strikes, major New York newspapers carried expensive full-page advertisements paid for by two groups who supported the union's version of the dispute. Indeed, in the midst of all of the public debate over due process, one ad was signed by twenty-five white liberal intellectuals under the rubric of the Ad Hoc Committee to Defend the Right to Teach.[21] The address listed was the same as that of the LID. The second was signed by black trade unionists solicited by the A. Philip Randolph Institute, whose executive director was Bayard Rustin. Both ads claimed that the issues were not racial. One, the Harrington ad, claimed that "The overwhelming majority of black teachers are supporting the UFT strike." The issue, it said, "is understood by black and white teachers alike—which explains their strong solidarity."[22] Although the public record illustrated this as "deliberate falsehood," this news was widely disseminated.[23] In fact, writes Stern, one week before these ads had appeared, a black caucus was organized within the UFT to oppose the strike. They issued a press release that had been signed by five of the six black members of the union's

executive board in addition to the only two black elected officials who had denounced the strike. Moreover, most of the
black teachers who stayed home during the May strikes said
later that they did so only because the union had received support for the supervisor's association to lock the schools. In
those areas where community and parent pressure could force
the opening of these schools, most, if not all, black teachers
had consistently reported for work.[24]

None of these ads mentioned the union's frantic lobbying
efforts against decentralizing legislation. The UFT appeared
in Albany passing out leaflets warning that local school districts would be operated under community control ". . . on the
basis of local prejudices based on color, race, or religion."[25]
They called those assemblymen who openly supported the
legislation "Black Power advocates," which was intended as an
insult. At one of their rallies in Albany, Shanker said to lobbying teachers, "If the Regents Bill passes I will follow every leg-
islator around who voted for it and kill them politically."[26]
Some legislators took this announcement very seriously, fearing that Shanker could in fact do this.

Jerry Kretchmer, a thirty-four-year-old assemblyman for
Manhattan's West Side, angrily recalled how fifty or sixty
teachers at a time would crowd into his office to berate him.
They warned that the bill was an invitation to unfolding chaos.
When he stood firm, the teachers threatened to campaign
against him. At one point he said, "If decentralization leads to
a year of chaos, I am prepared for it. *There's no education in the
schools anyway.*"[27] An infuriated teacher spat in the assemblyman's direction. What angered the UFT most about Kretchmer was that he supported decentralization as, what they
termed, an "independent." In other words, he was in favor of
such a legislative move even though he did not represent a predominantly black area.[28]

The UFT effectively managed to stampede the legislation.

The Marchi Bill that was passed delegated all power to the New York City Board of Education. The UFT had no fear of decisions located there.

Despite these gains for the union, Shanker said at the unions' delegate assembly before the Democratic primary when he returned, that the union would "... undertake an intensive campaign to support those legislators who supported its position in Albany and to defeat those who did not."[29] This move made union allies out of some of the state's most reactionary legislators. Why was Shanker so adamant?

The union had very strong chapters in Ocean Hill–Brownsville when the governing board took over in 1967. They were furious when the local board had chosen McCoy over their comrade and candidate Jack Bloomfield, principal of J.H.S. 271 introduced earlier in the anecdote in which students compared the atmosphere of their school under white and then black control. The suspicion of the local chapter intensified when the governing board had chosen five new principals (among them the first Chinese and Puerto Rican principals in New York City), none of whom appeared on the approved civil service list.[30] The Ocean Hill–Brownsville community's refusal to support the UFT's September strike had made things worse. When union teacher representatives resigned from their positions on the local board, no efforts had been made to negotiate their return.

For Albert Shanker, none of these actions surprised him. He saw Ocean Hill–Brownsville "as one battle in a larger war."[31] UFT Vice President John O'Neill described Shanker's thinking about the experimental district as follows:

> Shanker [had] a domino theory. He [thought] what happened in Ocean Hill–Brownsville [would] happen in thirty districts if it [wasn't] stopped there. His basic philosophy [was] power. If he [could] destroy Ocean Hill–

Brownsville, then no other district [would] try the same thing. They [wouldn't] try to exercise their power to hire and fire for fear the union [would] destroy them.[32]

Shanker saw job protection as his union's primary issue. He aspired to secure this protection, in spite of the community's desire to improve their children's quality of education by eliminating those people Shanker sought to protect. After a year of extended conflict in Ocean Hill–Brownsville, Shanker was forced to rethink the elements that constituted this notion of protection. Part of a teacher's protection surely involves the teacher's presence in a community in which he or she is actually wanted. Although O'Neill was the one to best describe Shanker's single-mindedness, he was soon to encounter it head on. O'Neill had been the only white member of the union's top staff to oppose the October strike designed to force the rehiring of transferred teachers in District 17 and instead proposed a compromise settlement. O'Neill, who was appalled by the idea of teachers being forced on to a community by police, had visited McCoy to discuss the prospects of negotiating a compromise. Although it was unclear how this would take place, both wished to avoid direct confrontation. When O'Neill called Shanker to discuss this prospect, Shanker said, "Fuck you. I want those teachers in the classroom now."[33] When O'Neill publicly denounced the threat of a third strike in October 1968, arguing instead for negotiations and compromise, he was called before the UFT's executive board and fired. Shanker made no pretenses of giving *de facto* recognition to the governing board through direct negotiations. His strategy instead, in the words of Stern, "was to cripple the entire system as leverage to force the mayor and the central Board to discipline and break the Ocean Hill–Brownsville board."[34]

Sol Stern argued that despite the calling for due process hearings for teachers and demands that the Ocean Hill–Brownsville board be suspended if it refused to rehire union teachers, the issue for the union was not due process, vigilantism, or anti-Semitism, but who would exercise power in the schools and who would make educational policy—elected community boards or the union. There was never any question that there were instances of anti-Semitism in a community responding to a school system run disproportionately by Jews. These issues, argued Stern, could not have been changed by the presence of police wielding their power. Instead, if the union had fought for strong decentralization with adequate safeguards for teachers in cooperation with the local board, they would have been better able to protect their own teachers in ghetto schools and their own ties with an ever-increasing black and Puerto Rican New York City school community. They might have also contributed to, rather than abated, efforts to bring more teachers and administrators of color into the public education field. But this did not happen. On the contrary, the UFT led the crusade against the community board, eventually demanding its dismantling as one of its primary points in strike negotiations. When the governing board ignored directives from the central Board to give returning teachers duties, the UFT agreed to a settlement that would be enforced by State Commissioner Allen. In addition to the return of the seventy-nine union teachers, a state supervisory committee would oversee teachers' rights. Ocean Hill–Brownsville would be governed by a state trustee. The governing board would be suspended until it complied and several staff would be returned to headquarters. Although the governing board was later reinstated, this was the beginning of the end. The UFT had portrayed black and Puerto Rican community efforts as at best extraneous and at worst an obstacle to effective class politics.

When one discusses progressive politics in public and academic discourse, it is assumed that one is describing the work of labor organizers and grass-roots community activists. Both forms are assumed, whether implicitly or explicitly, to be informed by Marxist theory: by a commitment to the eradication of the poverty of the working class and urban or rural poor through organized struggle and by a sharp critique of the capitalist order, which suggests that all efforts will be at best ameliorative with anything short of major economic restructuring. Although a body of influential literature to support this assumption about the theoretical bases of progressive and labor politics, neoliberal discourse on class perhaps best exemplified in the work of William Julius Wilson also abounds.[35]

Theorists like Wilson suggest that issues of class inequality can be adequately addressed under liberal capitalism through either an intensification of economic growth via market expansion or through the intervention of social welfare–state reforms, such as provisions for the creation of public jobs. Social theorists and critics like Wilson describe the intersection of race and class through analyses of the "underclass"—people who are structurally unemployable, or, in contemporary parlance, locked in a "culture of poverty." In both explanations, however, there is no systematic encounter with the ways in which cultural capital is racially designated; or the ways in which capitalism itself, as John Maynard Keynes has argued, is incapable of achieving full employment. This consideration is not intended to lead us into the morass of political economic literature. Instead, I simply wish to point out that class can be used as a center piece in political organizing, which is not itself progressive. Such charges, in fact, were made against the UFT. Can a labor organization be called "progressive" after it has identified itself with the interests of white- over blue-collar people?

Some observers of the Ocean Hill–Brownsville conflicts between the union and the governing board argued that the UFT's politics had remained unchanged over time and that it did not recognize its own anachronistic quality: Its supporters neither saw that the social, economic, and political realities of New York City had changed since the Old Left first began its theorizing, nor that discussing class as a singular category for emancipatory praxis was no longer adequate, and that such talk essentially led to the preservation and protection of the rights of middle-class over, and against, the needs of truly working-class people. Who, after all, were the working-class people in this situation? Clearly, they were those living in the community of Ocean Hill–Brownsville. Wrote Sol Stern:

> Today the situation is reversed: the success of the union in winning collective- bargaining rights for all teachers has made it the instrument of job security, and now the conservative and the mediocre have become the union's majority. Now it is the radicals who break the picket lines. It is the conservatives, afraid of the black community, panicked about their jobs, who shout "scab" at those who oppose the strike.[36]

In an informal interview with Stern, one of these "scabs," Sandra Adickes—an English teacher, who crossed the picket lines during the strike, joined parent groups to force the reopening of closed schools on the Lower East Side, walked the union's first picket lines and helped to organize the Mississippi freedom school—was, like many of the recently hired white and more experienced black teachers, leaving the union. She said:

I don't think the traditional trade union concept is any longer relevant. In six years the UFT has become middle-aged. When I started in 1960, it was relevant. We were making $4,800 a year and the union did a good job in improving conditions. But there's no pioneering trade union spirit here any more. It's all bread and butter, salaries and working conditions and job security. It used to be that young girls would teach for a few years hoping to marry a doctor or lawyer, but now they're marrying other teachers—you see them holding hands at meetings—and with two salaries they are really doing well. But their apathy is appalling. And now they're afraid of blacks and violence.[37]

Many of those opposed to the union formally resigned. Many others wished for an accounting of the large sums used to lobby in Albany. One defender of the union, Patrick Harnett, argued that the mayor and upper-middle-class intellectuals were placing undue blame on the teachers and their representative body—the UFT. He argued further that allegiance and identification with poor black communities was far easier for this higher class group of people who did not immediately feel the effects of black insurgency and struggles for economic and social justice. Harnett continued that such people despised the lower-middle-class ethos of most teachers who, in fact, had to deal with the results of their policymaking efforts. He wrote:

We hear the charge that teachers today are acting like "plumbers," that they are not "dedicated." What is interesting to me about these charges is not that they are false (there is much truth in them) but that if teachers act like this it should really be surprising to anybody. The public school teachers in this city are in the main a "lower-middle-class" group of people; that is, they reflect the values, thinking, goals, and lifestyle of a group of people whose parents were working class. They are people who did not have "things" and now want "things," the same things that everybody in our consumer culture wants—and if they have to act like members of an electricians' union to get them, they will.

"But shouldn't teachers be different?" people ask. Yes, certainly, I would respond. . . . But is there any reason to really expect the 55,000 school teachers of this city to measure up to these qualifications? . . . The New York City teacher is a member of an aspiring economic class first, and a teacher second. . . . Most important of all, in regard to the present struggle of black and Puerto Rican people for "local control," he does not feel that he is the singular perpetrator of education crimes committed against black and Puerto Rican children, and he therefore does not feel that he should be made the scapegoat to assuage the guilt felt by much more affluent whites over their much larger role in committing these crimes.[38]

Harnett argued that most New York City teachers were, by May 1968 acting out of fear. They had, he claimed, seen the "arbitrary dismissal of hundreds of teachers from their jobs . . . and that nobody really objects to it." He also asserted that when describing these turns as breaches of contract, the teachers were summarily dismissed as "racists." In this context, "honoring the contract" and "job security" became holy issues as whites aligned themselves against what they feared—"black power."[39]

The claim that the union teachers were not receiving public support against their treatment by the board seemed absurd to the newly employed teachers in Ocean Hill–Brownsville schools. The new teachers were to become the major antagonists of striking teachers in the months that followed. Wrote one such teacher, Charles Isaacs:

> The white teachers . . . in addition to being younger and better educated . . . have less experience in working for the system, and more in working against it, than any other faculty in the city. . . . [Nearly] all are "committed" to social changes. Many sections of the country are represented, as are most major colleges and universities. Alan Kellock, a teacher of Afro-American history, is writing a doctoral dissertation for the University of Wisconsin in that field; Sandy Nystrom is a former white organizer for the Mississippi Freedom Democratic Party; Stu Russell is a returned Peace Corps volunteer; Steve Bloomfield is an organizer of the Brooklyn Heights Peace and Freedom Party.[40]

These teachers, disdained by their older union colleagues for their youth, naivete, and seemingly obtuse political thinking, thought of the UFT as narrow, careerist, and self-interested. When the Board of Education ordered that these employees be returned to their schools along with a force of about three thousand armed police bodyguards in May 1968, the new teachers thought there would be no way to make the community or the faculty accept the teachers back with open arms.

The Board of Education stated:

> The governing board will act in good faith and their public assurance to the mayor at City Hall on Sunday will be honored. To the Board of Education this means that each teacher who wants to return to his former

school and to his professional assignment will not be prevented from doing so, and that these actions will be carried out in good faith and without reprisal.[41]

When the ten of the original nineteen who still wished to return to Ocean Hill–Brownsville and their dismissed supporters returned to J.H.S. 271, they were met by organized mobs of parents and individuals who Sonny Carson had organized to provide protection to the community. The teachers were escorted into the school building. They were scuttled into a room in which representatives of the local board and community representatives told them that they were not welcome, that the community wished that they would leave. The following day the same thing happened. This time, the returnees met with new teachers who said much the same as the community had. McCoy announced that he could not guarantee the safety of returning teachers. He also denied that he had ever promised that the teachers would be allowed to return to regular classroom duties. Meanwhile, the Board of Education approved an agreement with the UFT. Because no effective steps were taken to carry this agreement out, the UFT went back on a two-day strike. Yet another agreement was reached on September 29, 1968. The teachers were to be returned and observers from the Board of Education, UFT, and the mayor's office would accompany them. The local board had never accepted this agreement. The same group of parents gathered outside the schools and the board said that they, too, would send in observers. One of the observers said that when union teachers came back to school, much conflict ensued. Isaacs recounted:

Examples sound absurd when repeated. One of the UFT teachers for instance, walked into the middle of a math class I was teaching, marched to the center of the room, and began picking papers up off the floor. I asked: "What are you doing here? You're disrupting my class." In reply, he told me that he was not disrupting the class, but I was. Then, with the students (thirteen to fifteen years old) looking at him—their eyes filled, some with amazement, some with hatred, some with confusion—I walked toward the door, opened it for him, and told him to leave. He went to the door, but rather than leave, he started rummaging in the wastebasket, for no apparent reason. Finally, he straightened up, turned to the class, belched loudly and walked out. Barely containing myself, I slammed the door shut.

Presumably he had wanted to disrupt the class and provoke either me or a student into taking a swing at him. If so, he succeeded in his first objective, and almost succeeded in the second.

After he left the room, the students, miles from algebra by this time, released the accumulated tension by applauding and, after quieting down, they asked questions: "Why can't the kids take care of them?" "Why did they have to come back? Everything was so good." These questions may not display a high degree of political sophistication, but they certainly raise doubts as to whether teachers like the one who disrupted my class can ever be effective in one of our classrooms.[42]

Many new teachers could not believe the air of arrogance with which the UFT teachers carried themselves. It was described this way by Isaacs: "It's as though they're saying, 'We're back. We won. You lost. Ha! Ha! Ha!'"[43] The new teachers, facing the suspension of their own administrators, found this petty and obnoxious. They had also been informed by Superintendent Donovan that if there was an excess number of teachers in Ocean Hill–Brownsville, it would not be members of the union who would go without pay.

The UFT had, despite the premise of labor organizing, affiliated itself with a middle-class and lower-middle-class body of white-collar workers against a community of predominantly blue-collar and unemployed people of color. Part of the latter's goal was to enable their community educational resources to contribute to their economic upliftment as schools in other communities had done, including Jewish communities thirty years earlier.

While setting themselves up as posing *the challenge* to nationalistic politics, the union leaders obscured the fact that their own interests were narrowly formulated; they articulated their race interests as vital and black interests as extraneous and problematic. It should be remembered however, that not every member of the Jewish community shared this view. Indeed, Michael Walzer claimed that what he saw to be most awful about Ocean Hill–Brownsville was that it had produced a "civil war" amongst Jews.[44] This was clearest among the new and old teachers. Although the new group of teachers criticized claims of anti-Semitism as a phony cover-up and spoke out consistently in favor of their employers and the protections offered them, these were for the most part unheeded.

What must raise serious questions in our minds about the ultimate significance of charges of black anti-Semitism was the fate of the less-known experimental district, New Bridges, in Manhattan. New Bridges was the most ethnically diverse of the three experimental districts. The two largest groups were Chinese and Puerto Rican, with smaller numbers of U.S. blacks and whites. Although it failed ever really to get going because of continuing power struggles within the community, and therefore never received charges of the illegality of their work, it, too, was quickly disbanded by the Board of Education and labeled as an example of the parochialism that would infect local schools when left to the control of their own communities.

Conclusion

A Question of Whose Children Benefit from Whose Labor

In an interview, Paget Henry, former Chair of Afro-American Studies, Professor of Sociology at Brown University, and former student activist at City College of the City University of New York (CUNY), explained to me the ways in which the Open Admissions movement at City College in New York had grown directly out of fights for community control in Harlem.[1] Coming to New York City from Antigua at the age of eighteen, Henry had applied to his local public college, been admitted, and begun his studies. He thought nothing of it. It was a public university and his parents were taxpaying residents of the city. Henry explained that he soon realized that his own experience of admission and enrollment was, in fact, very unusual. When his younger brother, who had actually gone through the city's high school system applied to the local college, his application was rejected. This surprised Henry's family. After all, Henry had been educated on a small island in a second-world country in the Caribbean. His family figured his record would have been the one subject to suspicion. But his brother's?

Henry's family soon found out that his brother's experience was, in fact, a widespread phenomenon. Students from his brother's school and others throughout the city who had completed all of the necessary coursework to earn their high school diplomas, and who had performed reasonably well, were consistently being turned down by the CUNY colleges. The university had devised a system, much like many other universities, of weighing grades received from different New York City schools. "B" grades earned at ghetto or "600" schools were of different value than, for example, "C" grades earned at the magnet school, Bronx High School of Science. This strategy was based on the belief that different schools awarded grades on the basis of different expectations and standards of quality of student work. This policy led inevitably to the barring of a whole population of school students from the local university, which they and their families supported financially with their New York City income tax dollars. How, after all, were students to know that they were not doing what was required for admission to college when they were fulfilling all of their own school requirements? Surely one was supposed to lead to the other.

Many outraged members of Henry's community turned to the question of high school reform: How could they be re-invigorated so that they could offer the necessary preparation for continued education? Could they be changed and thus considered worthy enough in the eyes of the university admission officers? This group fought for integration and then local control, and for new programs and better-trained teachers. They confronted, at every turn, the intransigence of school bureaucracies described by Max Weber. Finally, determining that the transformation of public schools in urban communities of color was nearly impossible, Henry and fellow student activists turned their energies to their own school, City College.

If the successful completion of high school would not guarantee admission to public institutions of higher education, Henry argued, then City College's admission procedures needed to be changed. Henry and his fellow student activists argued that every city resident should be allowed equal opportunity to earn an inexpensive, quality Bachelor's degree. They did not claim that every student was equally prepared to go to college. Indeed, Henry's group demanded that Open Admissions be accompanied by a series of remedial programs designed to prepare "600" high school students for college-level work. Informing their political activity was the belief that people of color were not intrinsically or categorically of fewer intellectual abilities than whites, but that they had not been given the equivalent access to quality education that was their right. They had no doubt that when made available, students of color would be able to capitalize on such opportunities in the same, if not greater, proportion to their white counterparts.

In the midst of organizing the struggle for Open Admissions, Henry was approached by several members of the Harlem community. They offered to provide physical protection for him and his fellow student activists during their upcoming demonstrations. Henry refused. Why would they need protection? They were students at the university fighting for the rights of high school students to attend the college that they and their families supported financially. As Henry's group's activity escalated, however, they were met with increased police response. Harlem community members, Henry realized in retrospect, had anticipated such physical attacks, for when they had engaged in such activist work in the past, they too suffered consistent police brutality.

Eventually, the Open Admissions movement reaped success, but the policy has often been attacked for "lowering the standards of the university," and efforts to undermine its significance continue and intensify.

On December 23, 1999, for instance, CUNY Chancellor Matthew Goldstein, wrote a letter to members and friends of CUNY announcing three significant events that had transpired in the prior month: The New York State Board of Regents had approved CUNY's Master Plan Amendment to phase out remedial course work in the University's baccalaureate programs. This took effect in January 2000 for Baruch, Brooklyn, Queens, and Hunter Colleges, in September 2000 for John Jay, the College of Staten Island, and New York City Technical College, and in September 2001 for City, Lehman, York, and Medgar Evers Colleges. As of those dates, wrote Goldstein, "students [interested in enrolling in or transferring to a baccalaureate degree program would have to] demonstrate either by appropriate scores on the SAT, ACT, or Regent Exams, or on the University's diagnostic tests, that they [were] prepared to handle college-level work."[2]

In that same letter, Goldstein reported that the Board of Trustees voted to strengthen transfer policies to enable intra-University study and asked that the State of New York raise the University's funding by 7 percent to finance new faculty and academic support positions.

Together, argued Goldstein, these actions would support academic achievement and enhance the educational experience of CUNY students. Phasing out remedial courses would "liberate [these] resources," allowing the senior colleges to "focus their missions more sharply." This, in turn, would allow the community colleges to fulfill their historic roles. The emphasis on the distinction between the community and senior colleges would encourage the development of new ways to "work together as an integrated system." Baccalaureate programs could "begin at a higher level" while encouraging "the continuing support of all prospective students." Goldstein cited academic support programs already in place, including a pre-freshman summer skills immersion program.

The move to cut remedial courses, along with the enforced transfer plan would "lay the groundwork [for] improving quality at CUNY while enhancing access." The real work though, continued Goldstein, was still to come. He argued that the CUNY administration would need to find ways to "minimize dislocations from the phase-out of remedial work," and to encourage departments, programs, and faculty at each college to "work out [the] differences in curriculum between liberal arts and sciences courses at the senior and community colleges." These difference had, in the past, impeded transfers.

Goldstein then listed the programs that would be funded by the new monies: a CUNY Honors Academy, faculty recruitment and development, the Writing-Across-the-Curriculum Initiative, programs to assist high school students in preparing for college, and an Economic Development Program. While searching for four new college presidents, the assessment program for placing freshmen was being revamped through the use of "nationally honed instruments."

Goldstein concluded that he was not trying to recreate the University of thirty years past, but instead attempting to create a new sense of purpose, a "University that serves a more diverse student body at many skill levels, working toward many different goals." He continued:

> New Yorkers should see CUNY as a ladder spanning the distance from high school through college, graduate schools and post-professional training, as well as a resource for returning adults, for non-traditional students, and for the communities we serve. Students should be able to jump on and off the ladder at different stages of their lives, but at any time they should be able to climb as high as their dreams and talents will take them.

Goldstein then confessed that he too was a product of City College. From a family of limited means, the public University had been his "only hope for a better life." He was very appreciative of the high quality education he had received. Goldstein had been inspired by a sense of continuity, when he had witnessed the many obstacles students had had to overcome to attend the various CUNY campuses he visited. In this spirit, Goldstein closed, by urging that members of the CUNY community put their many different opinions about the appropriate new directions for the University aside so that they could "join hands and work together to shape a system in which all students [could] succeed."

The color of the communities served by the many campuses that comprise CUNY has changed dramatically in an atmosphere still marked by racial antagonism. The focus on color, however, tends to obscure the fact that the college has continued its historical mission of providing inexpensive education to the children of the urban poor and immigrants.[3] Still, the discourses on the challenges this project poses have shifted, as has the policy devised to address them. Educators know that deferring responsibility to the faculty for ensuring the smooth phasing out of remedial courses and the aligning of community and senior college classes is a clear, if cloaked announcement that the commitment to "high standards" will mean having to abandon the project of ensuring quality education for children from "600" schools and their contemporary equivalents. Even if individual faculty members try hard to support and encourage these students, the creation of an increased number of bureaucratic steps will easily decrease the enrollment of disenfranchised students. Furthermore, the "revamping" of placement tests for freshmen is really just another attempt at standardization through model exams like the SAT, now widely accepted as a test designed to measure familiarity with a particular set of test-taking skills. Few students from the communities discussed here have access to services like Kaplan, through which high school students can pay for exposure to requisite forms of knowledge.

Let us here return to the claims advanced by Hannah Arendt that blacks brought violence and demands for lower standards to college and university campuses and to Walzer's description of Black Power as a politics of "gesture." Perhaps we should now ask of them: Does it not seem ludicrous to speak of black violence when whites have effectively and violently cut off black access to most political options? Does it not seem equally disingenuous that when blacks demand the conditions that will allow them to cease "be[ing] the problem," they are accused of spreading antidemocratic racial division? Does not blaming black people for the "lowering of standards" obscure the systematic creation and preservation of situations that make learning for black students more arduous if not impossible? Why is it assumed that advocates of Black Power have been overtaken by adolescent anger and are acting without any theoretically or experientially informed political sensibilities? Would Walzer call the actions of the UFT or the white police Henry encountered "gestural"? Why is the fight of black people for what whites already possess not interpreted by more scholars as the fight of human beings for what should be considered as logical, understandable, and legitimate aspirations and needs?

Although the efforts of the community in Ocean Hill–Brownsville were not politically flawless, the experiment should have been allowed to exist. A critic might object to this and claim that if legislative allowances for community control make it possible for a Black Power school to exist, then a Ku Klux Klan school could argue for such a right as well. The difference between a Klan school and a Black Power school rests, however, on their constituency. Could one plausibly advance the position that U.S. schools have not been structured in favor of white students? Could one also plausibly advance the position that U.S. society offers fewer benefits for white students who complete their degrees under

the current condition? A Klan school openly denies participation of nonwhites, whereas a Black Power school, at least as
envisaged by the board of Ocean Hill–Brownsville aims to be
multiracial. (This is evidenced in their hiring of not only black,
but Chinese, Puerto Rican, and white principals and teachers
as well.) And finally, the Klan is, after all, a terrorist organization responsible for the maiming and deaths of many people
of color, as well as their white sympathizers, with near
impunity over the past century. It is absurd even to compare
black separatist groups, who lack such normative presump-
tions of reasonability, with the Klan.

Battles for community control by communities of color
have been more or less displaced by movement toward site-
based management and charter alternatives. Although some
individual leaders continue to take seriously what it means to
make their schools *of* these communities, more settle for vary-
ing degrees of race representation, with individual faculty or
administrators of color speaking on behalf of communities of
which they may or may not be a part.

Although well-intended, these measures are, in the end,
reformist. They do not represent a centralized commitment
to the use of public schools as places where the conditions of
inequity inflicting the the majority of people of color in the
United States may be altered. Such utilization of the schools
would require that the people who understand the situation
in the most sophisticated terms and who are genuinely com-
mited to transforming it, be allowed the power to reenvision
and recreate the relationship between public education and
U.S. democratic life. Reform of this nature would involve
more than just the employment of a certain number of
minorities, the rationing of courses that offer marginal treat-
ments of the history of people of color, and a small list of successful college students of color. It would require the creation

of a social and political reality in which the success of children of color is not deemed as the abnormal groping for unattainable standards of white normativity. This would require the ability to see in black people, dead and alive, a past with evidence of and future replete with greatness.

American public education is in crisis. Only communities like Ocean Hill–Brownsville, guided by civic duty instead of the nihilism of political apathy, will lead the way out. Efforts of the kind demonstrated by citizens of this community undeniably need the assistance of organized labor, which is also in crisis. It also needs those communities that the UFT rejected in Ocean Hill–Brownsville. Progress demands a reevaluation of the criteria used to determine the success and failure of political activity. We must allow innovative experiments, such as that begun in Ocean Hill–Brownsville, to continue long enough to generate tangible results.

Notes

Introduction

1. There are notable exceptions upon which I draw heavily throughout this book. These are best captured in Maurice R. Berube and Marilyn Gittell's *Confrontation at Ocean Hill–Brownsville: The New York School Strikes of 1968* (New York: Frederick A. Praeger, Publishers, 1969). My goal in what follows is to transform the insights in these shorter articles into a larger narrative of contemporary relevance.

2. Tom Cowan and Jack Maguire, *Timelines of African-American History: 500 Years of Black Achievement* (New York: A Roundtable Press, 1994), 254–64.

Chapter 1: Who Should Run the Schools?

1. Allan C. Ornstein, Daniel U. Levine, and Doxey A. Wilkerson, *Reforming Metropolitan Schools* (Pacific Palisades, CA: Goodyear Publishing Company, Inc., 1975), 112–13.

2. Ornstein et al., 113.

3. Ibid., 113.

4. Ibid., 114.

5. David Tyack, "School Governance in the United States: Historical Puzzles and Anomalies," in Jane Hannaway and Martin Carnoy, eds., *Decentralization and School Improvement: Can We Fulfill the Promise?* (San Francisco: Jossey-Bass Publishers, 1993), 1.

6. W. D. Farnham, "The Weakened Spring of Government: A Study in Nineteenth-Century American History," *American Historical Review* 68 (1963): 662–80 as cited in Tyack, 1.

7. F. Adams, *The Free School System of the United States* (Lon-

don: Chapman and Hall, 1875); E. D. Mansfield, *American Education, Its Principles and Elements* (New York: Barnes, 1851) as cited in Tyack, 5.

8. J. G. March and J. P. Olsen, "The New Institutionalism: Organizational Factors in Political Life," *American Political Science Review* 78 (1984): 734–49 as cited in Tyack, 5.

9. D. Tyack, R. Lowe, and E. Hansot, *Public Schools in Hard Times: The Great Depression and Recent Years* (Cambridge, MA: Harvard University Press, 1984) as cited in Tyack.

10. Richard Elmore, "School Decentralization: Who Gains? Who Loses?," in *Decentralization and School Improvement* (San Francisco: Jossey-Bass Publishers, 1993), 34 (see chapter 1 n. 5).

11. Ibid., 34.

12. Ibid., 35.

13. Ibid., 35.

14. Ibid., 35.

15. There are efforts to study results of student learning under changed structural arrangements. See, for example, Anthony S. Bryk, *Charting Chicago School Reform: Democratic Localism as a Lever for Change* (Boulder, CO: Westview Press, 1998) and Theodore R. Sizer, *Horace's School: Redesigning the American High School* (Boston: Houghton Mifflin Company, 1992).

16. Elmore, 35.

17. Ibid., 35.

18. Ibid., 35–36.

19. Ibid., 36.

20. Ibid., 36.

21. Ibid., 36.

22. This phrase comes from Enrique Dussel's now canonical work by that name, *The Underside of Modernity: Apel, Ricouer, Rorty, Taylor, and the Philosophy of Liberation,* translated with

an introduction by Eduardo Mendieta (New York: Prometheus Books/Humanity Books, 1996).

23. See, for example, Stokely Carmichael (Kwame Ture) and Charles V. Hamilton, *Black Power: The Politics of Liberation in America* (New York: Random House, 1967).

24. Ornstein et al.

25. See, for instance, Ornstein et al., 116–19. These authors created an extraordinarily useful chart that outlines arguments for and against community control.

26. Ornstein et al., 116–19. See also Patrick Harnett, "Why Teachers Strike: A Lesson for Liberals," in Maurice R. Berube and Marilyn Gittell, eds., *Confrontation at Ocean Hill–Brownsville: The New York School Strikes of 1968* (New York: Frederick A. Praeger Publishers, 1969), 211.

27. My outline of these arguments for and against community control is taken entirely from the chart mentioned in chap. 1, n. 22. See Ornstein et al., 116–19. For discussion of continued discrimination, see Douglas S. Massey and Nancy A. Dentin, *American Apartheid: Segregation and the Making of the Underclass* (Cambridge, MA: Harvard University Press, 1993) and William G. Bowen and Derek Bok, in collaboration with James L. Shulman, Thomas I. Nygren, Stacy Berg Dale, and Lauren A. Meserve, *The Shape of the River: Long-Term Consequences of Considering Race in College and University Admissions* (Princeton, NJ: Princeton University Press, 1998).

28. On parents' efforts to find good alternative educational resources for their children, see Maurice R. Berube, "The Unschooling of New York Children," in *Confrontation at Ocean Hill–Brownsville*, 136–39, and Ornstein et al., 116–19.

29. For discussion of the white bias in professional examinations and other modes of social assessment, see Charles S. Isaacs, "A JHS 271 Teacher Tells It Like He Sees It," 195, and Fred Feretti, "Who's to Blame in the School Strike?," 285, both in *Confrontation at Ocean Hill–Brownsville*; Bowen and Bok,

The Shape of the River and Gertrude Ezorsky, *Racism and Justice: The Case for Affirmative Action* (Ithaca: Cornell University Press, 1991).

30. For critique of the fiscal thesis, see Ornstein et al., 116–19.

31. For discussion of these claims for community control, see Ornstein et al., 116–19, and Rhody McCoy, "The Year of the Dragon," in *Confrontation at Ocean Hill–Brownsville*, 52–63.

32. For the critical response of the community of experts, see *Decentralization and School Improvement*.

33. For criticisms based on white flight from and black stratification in the cities, see William J. Wilson, *The Truly Disadvantaged: The Inner City, the Underclass, and Public Policy* (Chicago: University of Chicago Press, 1987).

34. Max Weber, *From Max Weber: Essays on Sociology*, trans. with an intro. by H. H. Gerth and C. Wright Mills (New York: Oxford University Press, 1946), 196f.

35. Ibid., 214.

36. Ibid., 215.

37. Ibid., 215–16.

38. Ibid., 221.

39. Ibid., 239.

40. For discussion of the emergence of the dichotomy between the public and private, see Hannah Arendt, *The Human Condition* (Chicago: University of Chicago Press, 1958), 22–73.

41. Weber, 216.

42. Ibid., 221.

43. Ibid., 224.

44. Ibid., 240, 243.

45. Ibid., 228.

46. Because there was not such a sharp discrepancy in the racial demographics of the populations of students and staff in suburban schools, particular and episodic issues might have caused disagreement and dissension, but there was not a prevailing and omnipresent sense on the part of school employ-

ees that the children in the schools were fundamentally "other people's children." White normativity, in other words, unified those who controlled and those who inhabited the schools.

47. See, for example, Michael Harrington, "The Freedom to Teach: Beyond the Panaceas," in *Confrontation at Ocean Hill–Brownsville*, 129–39, for discussion of those who saw the move to community control as a perversion of decentralization. And for those who were simply embarrassed by it, see Maurice J. Goldbloom, "The New York School Crisis," in *Confrontation at Ocean Hill–Brownsville*, 271.

Chapter 2: Black Power

1. C. L. R. James, "Black Power" in Anna Grimshaw, ed. *C. L. R. James Reader* (Oxford, UK and Cambridge, MA: Blackwell, 1993), 362.

2. Ibid., 367.

3. Ibid., 368.

4. William L. Van Deburg, ed. *Modern Black Nationalism: From Marcus Garvey to Louis Farrakhan* (New York: New York University Press, 1997), 10–13.

5. Stokely Carmichael (Kwame Ture) and Charles V. Hamilton (see chapter 1, n. 23).

6. Ibid., 10.

7. Ibid., 18–20.

8. Ibid., 167.

9. *The Autobiography of Malcolm X*, as told by Alex Haley (New York: Ballantine Books, 1964), 381.

10. J. Edgar Hoover, "Memorandum to Special Agent in Charge, Albany, New York, August 25, 1967," reprinted in Van Deburg's *Modern Black Nationalism*, 134.

11. Ibid., 134.

12. See Annie Stein, "Containment and Control: A Look at the Record," in Annette T. Rubenstein, ed. *Schools Against Chil-*

dren: The Case for Community Control (New York: Monthly Review Press, 1970), 48–49, for discussion of the 1966 school year and I.S. 201.

13. See Annie Stein, 1970.

14. For demographics and discussion of the boycott, see Annie Stein, 1970.

15. For demographics of New York City between 1950 and 1960, see Richard Elmore, 46. See also Philip Kasinitz, *Caribbean New York: Black Immigrants and the Politics of Race* (Ithaca and London: Cornell University Press, 1992).

16. See Annie Stein (1970) for discussion of the City Wide Committee.

17. Although Annie Stein records (1970) that the scrawled signs read "Blacks go home!," after speaking with young black adults living in New York City during this period, it seems more likely that these signs would have read, "Niggers go home!"

18. For more discussion of this first transfer attempt, see Stein, 1970.

19. For discussion of the second aim of the City Wide Committee, black and Puerto Rican responses, and the board's response, see Stein, 1970.

20. See Stein, 1970.

21. For demographics of Brooklyn, see Earl Lewis, "The Need to Remember: Three Phases in Black and Jewish Educational Relations," in Jack Salzman and Cornel West, eds. *Struggles in the Promised Land: Toward a History of Black–Jewish Relations in the United States* (Oxford: Oxford University Press, 1997), 245, and Philip Kasinitz's *Caribbean New York*, especially chap. 2.

22. Richard Karp, "School Decentralization in New York," in *Confrontation at Ocean Hill–Brownsville*, 64.

23. Diane Ravitch, *The Great School Wars, New York City 1805–1973: A History of the Public Schools as Battlefield of Social Change* (New York: Basic Books, Inc., Publishers, 1974), 231.

24. Karp, 65.
25. Ravitch, 321.
26. Ibid., 314.
27. Eugenia Kemble, "Ocean Hill–Brownsville," in *Confrontation at Ocean Hill–Brownsville*, 34.
28. See Karp, 67.
29. Ibid., 66.
30. Ravitch, 315.
31. See, for instance, Karp, 66.
32. Cited in Kemble, 35.
33. Board of Education Policy Statement on Decentralization, adopted by the New York City Board of Education in public session, April 19, 1967.
34. I found out about the "600" school designation through an interview with Dennis Littky, Co-Principal of the Metropolitan Career and Vocational Center in Providence Rhode Island, and former coordinator of an alternative reading program at Ocean Hill–Brownsville in 1969. Six hundred was the number reserved for schools located in economically blighted neighborhoods of color. Paget Henry, former Chair of Afro-American Studies and Professor of Sociology at Brown University, described in our interview the ways in which the "600" school designation served as a criterion for rejecting applicants to the City University of New York (CUNY). That a degree could be earned for a total of $40 at the time at CUNY, made this practice a particularly egregious one since the populations excluded were the poorest in the city and the people who sought upward mobility through higher education. In effect, protested Henry, their tax dollars were being used to fund the education of other, often economically better off, people.
35. For more on McCoy, see Fred Ferretti, "Who's to Blame in the School Strike?," in *Confrontation at Ocean Hill–Brownsville*, 284–85. My description comes from Jonathan Kaufman, "Blacks and Jews: The Struggle in the Cities," in *Struggles in the Promise Land*, 113 and Ravitch, 322.

36. Kaufman, 113.

37. Karp, 68.

38. The anonymous onlooker was cited in the Niemeyer Report: "An Evaluative Study of the Process of School Decentralization in New York City," the Final Report by the Advisory and Evaluation Committee on Decentralization to the Board of Education of the City of New York (July 30, 1968) included in *Confrontation at Ocean Hill–Brownsville*, 37. The Niemeyer Committee was assigned to evaluate the progress of the experiment at Ocean Hill–Brownsville.

39. See Niemeyer Report.

40. Ravitch, 323.

41. Ibid., 324.

42. McCoy, 53.

43. Ibid., 53.

44. For discussion of the governing board's responses, see Ira Glasser, "The Burden of the Blame: NYCLU [New York Civil Liberties Union] Report on the Ocean Hill–Brownsville School Controversy," in *Confrontation at Ocean Hill–Brownsville*, 108. Hereafter cited as "The NYCLU Report."

45. Goldbloom, 251 (see chap. 1, n. 47).

46. Ravitch, 325.

47. McCoy, 54.

48. Ibid.

49. Kemble, 36.

50. See Niemeyer Report.

51. Excerpted from a written statement by the seven UFT chapter chairmen of schools participating in the experimental district and a number of teacher representatives to the planning board as cited in Kemble, 37.

52. For discussion of the bigoted teachers, see "Statement by the

Teachers of the Ocean Hill–Brownsville Experimental District" (September 27, 1967), cited in the Niemeyer Report.

53. "Statement by the Teachers of the Ocean Hill–Brownsville Experimental District."

54. McCoy, 56.

55. Ravitch, 326.

56. Ibid., 336.

57. Cited in Ravitch, 326. Although it was old news to members of the black community, COINTELPRO documents made public in 1971 revealed a state policy to criminalize black activist leaders. Of course black criminals do exist, but there is a long history of police planting and government offices manufacturing materials to make innocent activists of color appear guilty.

58. For discussion, see Goldbloom, 259, and Ravitch, 327.

59. Ravitch, 327.

60. Ibid.

61. Ibid.

62. Karp, 70.

63. Maurice R. Berube and Marilyn Gittell, "The Struggle for Community Control," in *Confrontation at Ocean Hill–Brownsville*, 15.

64. For more on Shanker, see Sol Stern, "'Scab' Teachers," in *Confrontation at Ocean Hill–Brownsville*, 182. This description comes from Ravitch, 317–18.

65. See *Confrontation at Ocean Hill–Brownsville*.

66. McCoy, 58.

67. Ibid., 59.

68. Karp, 70.

69. See, for example, Charles S. Isaacs, 201.

70. See the Niemeyer Report.

71. See the NYCLU Report.

72. Karp, 69–70.
73. See Ravitch, 353.
74. For discussion of McCoy asking Shanker to set up a committee of teachers in the district to prepare proposals for new programs, see Ravitch, 339.
75. "Questions by the Teachers Who Are Teaching in the Ocean Hill–Brownsville Demonstration Project, Addressed to Mr. McCoy, the Unit Administrator, and Members of the Governing Board" (December 1967), Special Collection of the Politics and Education Program at Teacher's College in Ravitch, 339. See also Eugenia Kemble, "New York Experiments in School Decentralization," *The United Teacher* (December 20, 1967).
76. See the Niemeyer Report.
77. For the demonstration principles, see Ravitch, 345.
78. See Karp, 70.
79. Ibid.
80. Ibid., 70–71.
81. Ibid., 71.
82. Ibid.
83. Ibid.
84. Ibid.
85. Ibid.
86. McCoy, 59.
87. Ibid.
88. Ravitch, 345.
89. Ibid., 346.
90. Ibid., 346.
91. Karp, 72.
92. Ravitch, 397.
93. Ibid., 351.
94. See NYCLU Report.

95. For discussion, see Isaacs, 202–5.
96. See Stern, 183–86.

Chapter 3: White Power

1. Julius Lester, *Lovesong: Becoming a Jew* (New York: Arcade Publishing, 1988), 48.
2. Isaacs, 202.
3. Stern, 176–77 (see chap. 2, n. 64).
4. Ibid.
5. Stern, 179. To speak of "militancy" in labor politics is almost required to signal one's authenticity and seriousness as an activist and as a leader. Although many black activists had grown tired of playing down the seriousness of their political work, they knew that to bring together the words "black" and "militancy" was enough to inspire fear, doubt, and dread in many white and black onlookers.
6. Sandra Adickes, quoted by Sol Stern, 182. Many efforts to create equity in hiring practices have revealed the mediocrity that unjust employment practices have allowed white employees. Although many who are antagonistic to efforts to increase the number of minority employees have suggested frequently that this work would require the lowering of standards, many who have worked on the other side know the opposite extreme to be the case: Because the system is so stacked against people of color, those who eventually are able to find work tend to be superb or awful. Mediocrity is the luxury afforded whites through their normativity.
7. Isaacs, "A JHS 271 Teacher Tells It Like He Sees It," 204 (see chap. 1, n. 29).
8. Ibid.
9. Ibid.
10. Whether this is in fact the case is not entirely clear. Liberal blacks and Jews and radical blacks and Jews have historically

formed coalitions and continue to do so in the present. Although there is a declining number of Jews on the left, the group that remains still represents a disproportionate number of the whites involved in such activity.

11. Kaufman, "Blacks and Jews," 112 and 116 (see chap. 2, n. 35).

12. Claybourne Carson, "Black-Jewish Universalism in the Era of Identity Politics," in *Struggles in the Promised Land*, 191.

13. Paul Buhle and Robin Kelley, "Allies of a Different Sort," *Struggles in the Promise Land*, 217.

14. Earl Lewis, "The Need to Remember," *Struggles in the Promise Land*, 247.

15. James Baldwin, "Negroes are Anti-Semitic Because They're Anti-White," in Nat Hentoff, ed. *Black Anti-Semitism and Jewish Racism*, 9.

16. See Norman Finkelstein's *The Holocaust Industry* (London: Verso, 2000) and his discussion of the manufacturing of the need to remember this historical disaster in particular ways, which were very profitable for a small set of Jewish elites over and against other suffering populations, including Holocaust survivors themselves.

17. Baldwin, 4. Still, this more humanistic point directs us to the important distinction made by Black Power advocates and the community in Ocean Hill–Brownsville, i.e., the difference between the structural position of white Jews and the white Jewish individual.

18. Ibid., 9. Quite the opposite. As Finkelstein has convincingly argued, the militarism of Israelis—many of them white American Jewish emigrants—became, in a complex twist of events, the active demonstration of their conservative, American patriotism.

19. Ibid., 10. Assimilationism is a contractual process, filled with the bad faith that is symptomatic of efforts to constantly prove one's authenticity. As Anna Goldberg, former Provost

of Wheaton College, so brilliantly put it, "Converts often become zealots."

20. Ibid., 10. I wish that advocates of reformism would rid political discourse of this inhumane mantra disguised as rational and level-headed argument once and for all. It is put forward without even a suggestion of its absurdity, as if disenfranchised people had nine lives or as if there is a predestined relationship between progressive political change and the steady and continuous movement of time.

21. Ibid., 8.

22. See E. D. Morel, *The Black Man's Burden: African Colonial Labor on the Congo and Ubangi Rivers, 1880–1900* (Boulder, CO: Westview Press, 1969) and Eric Hobsbawm, *The Age of Empire, 1875–1914* (New York: Pantheon Books, 1987). My husband and I heard a terrifying announcement on South African television. When advertising a British Broadcasting Channel show, it listed the percentages of the world's population living on each continent. Africa was said to contribute 8 percent. This is shocking, especially given that 100 hundred percent of the human population was once on the continent of Africa. Still, the ongoing assault on the continent— through colonization, conquest, bloody decolonization efforts, and all that followed—must have a cumulative effect. The continuous nature of this onslaught seems to pass unnoticed, save in opportunities to mention the brutality of the Africans.

23. Baldwin, 8.

24. Ibid., 11.

25. Ibid., 12.

26. For a recent critique of color-blind liberalism, see Amy Gutmann's contribution to her and Kwame Anthony Appiah's *Color Conscious: The Political Morality of Race* (Princeton: Princeton University Press, 1996).

27. I differentiate individual blacks from blacks as a group

since liberalism often tries, as President Clinton has in his withdrawal of Lani Guinier's nomination for Assistant Attorney General argued, that individuals should be addressed over groups. Guinier's work points out that the issue isn't black individuals—who always serve as exceptions to the rule of American anti-black racism—but blacks as a people, as a group against whom the nation's institutions and sociological environment discriminate. See Lani Guinier, *Tyranny of the Majority* (New York: The Free Press, 1994).

28. Consultation of Thomas Jefferson's *Notes on Virginia* (1787) in Merrill D. Peterson, ed. *The Writings of Thomas Jefferson* (New York: The Library of America, 1984). See also Appiah and Gutmann's discussions in *Color Conscious*.

29. See Colin A. Palmer, *Passageways: An Interpretive History of Black America*, Vol. II: 1863–1965 (New York: Harcourt Brace College Publishers, 1998), chapters 11 and 12.

30. Hannah Arendt, *On Violence* (New York: Harcourt Brace Javanovich, 1969), 18–19.

31. See Ornstein et al., *Reforming Metropolitan Schools*, 116–19.

32. Michael Walzer, "Blacks and Jews: A Personal Reflection," in *Struggles in the Promised Land*, 403. Walzer here appears to overlook the firm roots Black Power had in Pan-Africanism. Though the efforts of this movement were localized, they were to be simultaneous with other localized efforts worldwide. These were first steps in a much larger Third World movement.

33. Think, for example, of the group who gathered around Malcolm X. It included Japanese-American activist and resident of Harlem Yuri Koshiama. For African American–Asian American dynamics, see Joy Ann James, *Resisting State Violence in U.S. Culture* (Minneapolis: University of Minnesota Press, 1996), 15.

34. See Earl Lewis, 255, n. 51; Charles Isaacs, 202; and "Anti-Semitism—A Statement by the Teachers of Ocean Hill–Brownsville to the People of New York," in *Confrontation at Ocean Hill–Brownsville*, 170–71. For more on COINTEL-PRO, see Cedric J. Robinson, *Black Movements in America* (New York and London: Routledge, 1997), 151–52. See also Joy James's *Resisting State Violence*.

35. Pamphlet reprinted in *Confrontation at Ocean Hill–Brownsville*, 166.

36. Dwight MacDonald, "An Open Letter to Michael Harrington," *Confrontation at Ocean Hill–Brownsville*, 224.

37. Isaacs, 202.

38. Stern, 180.

39. Isaacs, 198.

40. Maurice R. Berube and Marilyn Gittell, "Anti-Semitism and Racism," in *Confrontation at Ocean Hill–Brownsville*, 164.

41. This is a reprint of the union-altered document. See *Confrontation at Ocean Hill–Brownsville*, 169.

42. Quoted in Lewis R. Gordon, "Introduction: Black Existential Philosophy," in Lewis R. Gordon, ed. with an intro., *Existence in Black: An Anthology of Black Existential Philosophy* (New York and London: Routledge, 1997), 2.

43. Describing his program's title, Julius Lester wrote: "The show's title is intended as self- mockery. But in the humorless atmosphere of the late Sixties it is taken seriously," *Lovesong*, 47.

44. Julius Lester, 50.

45. Ibid., 51.

46. Ibid., 55.

47. Ibid., 56.

48. Ibid.

49. Ibid., 56–57.

Chapter 4: When Some Workers Don't Look Toward the Left

1. Robert Rossner, *The Year Without an Autumn* (New York: Richard W. Baron, 1969), 213–14.
2. Patrick Harnett, 210–11.
3. Buhle and Kelly, 217 (see chap. 3, n. 13).
4. Kaufman, "Blacks and Jews," 112 (see chap. 2, n. 35).
5. Cornel West has raised the same criticism of liberal structuralists' failure to contend adequately with questions of nihilism in poor black communities. See his *Race Matters* (Boston: Beacon Press, 1993), chapter 1. For a discussion of West's passive nihilism, see Lewis R. Gordon in George Yancy's forthcoming volume on the thought of Cornel West.
6. Stern, 191 (see chap. 2, n. 64).
7. The NYCLU Report, 115, (see chap. 2, n. 41).
8. Ibid., 116.
9. Ibid., 117.
10. Ibid., 113.
11. Isaacs, 202 (see chap. 1, n. 29).
12. Kaufman, 114.
13. Ibid.
14. Stern, 181.
15. Ibid.
16. Ibid.
17. Ibid. Although beyond the scope of this chapter, it deserves mention that two, fundamentally different, groups socialists of all varieties and communists of all varieties, are often lumped together. One of the central differences is that communists see socialism as a stage in the revolutionary process, whereas socialists see socialism as the end goal. They often define themselves through their vehement anti-communism. It should not, therefore, strike us as surprising when we see the easy alliances that formed between the conservative socialists here and a small set of liberal intellectuals. Though both maintain a critical stance toward the present and

toward each other, the criticisms and actions of both are, in the end, reformist.

18. MacDonald, 227, (see chap. 3, n. 36).

19. Stern, 182.

20. In response to Nat Hentoff's claim that the ad should have been signed by the LID, Michael Harrington claimed that although some of the signatories were associated with that organization, others were not. The ad hoc committee was founded so that the working group was not limited to the commitments of a particular organization. Michael Harrington, "The Freedom to Teach: Beyond the Panaceas," in *Confrontation at Ocean Hill–Brownsville*, 130.

21. Reprinted in *Confrontation at Ocean Hill–Brownsville*, 120–22.

22. Ibid.

23. Stern, 183.

24. Ibid.

25. Ibid., 183–86.

26. Ibid., 185.

27. Ibid.

28. Ibid.

29. Ibid.

30. Ibid., 189.

31. Ibid.

32. Ibid.

33. Ibid., 190.

34. Ibid.

35. The body of literature on class is vast. For a discussion of its intersection with race—especially with regard to racism in labor organizing—see Philip Foner, *Organized Labor and the Black Worker, 1619–1973* (New York: International Publishers, 1976); Colin Palmer, *Passageways* 62, 164–65 (see chap. 3, n. 29). For neoliberal discussions of class, see William J. Wilson's *The Truly Disadvantaged* and Bill E. Lawson, ed. *The Underclass Question* (Philadelphia: Temple University Press, 1992).

36. Stern, 181.

37. Stern quoting Sandra Adickes, 181.
38. Patrick Harnett, 211.
39. Ibid.
40. Isaacs, 199.
41. Goldbloom, 276–77 (see chap. 1, n. 47).
42. Isaacs, 201.
43. Ibid.
44. Michael Walzer, 204 (see chap. 3, n. 32). Recall in my acknowledgment of my Rabbi, Arnold Jacob Wolf that he was among the Jewish leaders who crossed the picket line at Ocean Hill–Brownsville. Former Rabbi of K.A.M. Isaiah Israel Synagogue on the south side of Chicago, Rabbi Wolf is a scathing critic of liberalism. When addressing a predominantly liberal Jewish congregation on the eve of a Rosh Hashanah service, he observed: "Liberals are never there when you need them. They're always there when you don't."

Conclusion

1. Interview with Paget Henry, conducted by the author, December 2, 1998, at Brown University.
2. Thanks are due to Gary Schwartz, Program Director of the Lehman Scholars Program at CUNY, for drawing my attention to and providing me with a copy of this letter. His efforts clearly illustrate the possibility of an alternative future for CUNY, one that does not require that first-rate education be at odds with the education of students of color.
3. For a portrait of City College's history of serving immigrant communities—especially white Eastern European Jewish immigrants—see Morris Cohen's *A Dreamer's Journey: The Autobiography of Morris Raphael Cohen* (Boston: Beacon Press, 1949). Cohen's account of his activities while a student at City College, as well as those of his fellow Jewish activists as they struggled together to develop increased access to City College, are similar to Henry's.

Works Consulted

"Anti-Semitism?—A Statement by the Teachers of Ocean Hill–Brownsville to the People of New York." 1969. In *Confrontation at Ocean Hill–Brownsville: The New York School Strikes of 1968*, ed. M. Berube and M. Gittel. New York: Frederick A. Praeger, Publishers.

Appiah, Kwame Anthony and Amy Gutmann. 1996. *Color Conscious: The Political Morality of Race*. Princeton: Princeton University Press.

Arendt, Hannah. 1958. *The Human Condition*. Chicago: The University of Chicago Press.

———. 1969. *On Violence*. New York: Harcourt Brace Jovanovich.

Baldwin, James. 1962. *The Fire Next Time*. New York: Dell Publishing Company.

———. 1969. "Negroes Are Anti-Semitic Because They're Anti-White." In *Black Anti-Semitism and Jewish Racism*, ed. Nat Hentoff. New York: Richard W. Baron Publishing Company, pp. 3–12.

Begley, Sharon. 1995. Three Is Not Enough: Surprising New Lessons from the Controversial Science of Race. *Newsweek*, 13 February, 67–69.

Bell, Daniel. 1973. *The Coming of Post-Industrial Society*. New York: Basic Books.

———. 1976. *The Cultural Contradictions of Capitalism*. New York: Basic Books.

Bell, Derrick. 1992. *Faces at the Bottom of the Well: The Permanence of Racism*. New York: Basic Books.

Berube, Maurice and Marilyn Gittel, eds. 1969a. *Confrontation at Ocean Hill–Brownsville: The New York School Strikes of 1968*. New York: Frederick A. Praeger Publishers.

———. 1969b. "The Struggle for Community Control." In *Confrontation at Ocean Hill–Brownsville*, pp. 3–10.

Berube, Maurice. 1969. "The Unschooling of New York Children." In *Confrontation at Ocean Hill–Brownsville*, pp. 136–39.

Bowen, William G. and Derek Bok, in collaboration with James L. Shulman, Thomas I. Nygren, Stacy Berg Dale, and Lauren A. Meserve. 1998. *The Shape of the River: Long-Term Consequences*

of Considering Race in College and University Admissions.
Princeton: Princeton University Press.

Brazier, Arthur M. 1969. *Black Self-Determination: The Story of the Woodlawn Organization.* Grand Rapids, MI: William B. Eerdmans Publishing Company.

Brown, Daniel J. 1990. *Decentralization and School-Based Management.* New York and London: The Falmer Press.

Brotz, Howard M. 1970. *The Black Jews of Harlem: Negro Nationalism and the Dilemmas of Negro Leadership.* New York: Schocken Books.

Brown v. Board of Education of Topeka Kansas. 1954. 347 U.S. Supreme Court 483.

Bryke, Anthony S. 1998. *Charting Chicago Reform: Democratic Localism as a Lever for Change.* Boulder, CO: Westview.

Buhle, Paul and Robin Kelly. 1997. "Allies of a Different Sort." In *Struggles in the Promised Land: Toward a History of Black–Jewish Relations in the United States,* ed. Jack Salzman and Cornel West. Oxford: Oxford University Press, pp. 117–229.

Carmichael, Stokley, and Charles V. Hamilton. 1967. *Black Power: The Politics of Liberation in America.* New York: Random House.

Carson, Claybourne. 1997. "Black–Jewish Universalism in the Era of Identity Politics." In *Struggles in the Promised Land,* pp. 177–96.

Cary, Lorene. 1991. *Black Ice.* New York: Vintage Books.

Cohen, Morris Raphael. 1949. *A Dreamer's Journey: The Autobiography of Morris Raphael Cohen.* Boston: Beacon Press.

Comer, James and Alvin Poussaint. 1975. *Black Childcare: How to Bring up a Black Child in America.* New York: Pocketbooks.

Cowan, Tom and Jack Maguire. 1994. *Timelines of African-American History: 500 Years of Black Achievement.* New York: A Roundtable Press.

Cruse, Harold. 1984. *The Crisis of the Negro Intellectual: A Historical Analysis of the Failure of Black Leadership.* New York: Quill.

Daughtry, Herbert D. 1997. *No Monopoly on Suffering: Blacks and Jews in Crown Heights (and Elsewhere).* Trenton, NJ, and Asmara, Eritrea: Africa World Press, Inc.

Du Bois, W. E. B. 1898. "The Study of the Negro Problems." *Annals of the American Academy of Political and Social Sciences* 11 (January); reprinted in *The Black Sociologists.* (See Bracey, Meier, and Rudwick.)

———. 1982. *The Souls of Black Folk.* Intros. by Dr. Nathan Hare and Alvin Poussaint, M.D. Revised and updated bibliography. New York: New American Library. [Originally published in 1903.]

Duster, Troy. 1994. "Human Genetics, Evolutionary Theory, and Social Stratification." In *The Genetic Frontier: Ethics, Law, and Policy*, ed. M. S. Frankel and A. H. Teich. Washington, DC: American Association for the Advancement of Science.

Edwards, Ralph and Charles V. Willy. 1998. *Black Power/White Power in Public Education*. London: Praeger.

Elmore, Richard. 1993. "School Decentralization: Who Gains? Who Loses?" In *Decentralization and School Improvement: Can We Fulfill the Promise?*, ed. J. Hannaway and M. Carnoy. San Francisco: Jossey-Bass Publishers, pp. 33–54.

Ezorsky, Gertrude. 1991. *Racism and Justice: The Case for Affirmative Action*. Ithaca: Cornell University Press.

Fanon, Frantz. 1952. *Peau noire, masques blancs*. Paris: Editions de Seuil.

———. 1961. *Les damnés de la Terre*. Préface de Jean-Paul Sartre, présentation de Gérard Chaliand. Paris: François Maspero éditeur S.A.R.L.; Paris: Éditions Gallimard, 1991.

———. 1963. *The Wretched of the Earth*. Preface by Jean-Paul Sartre, trans. Constance Farrington. New York: Grove Press.

———. 1967a. *Black Skin, White Masks*. Trans. Charles Lam Markmann. New York: Grove Press.

———. 1967b. *Toward the African Revolution*, trans. Haakon Chevalier. New York: Grove Press.

———. 1979. *Pour la révolution africaine: écrits politiques*. Paris: François Maspero.

Farnham, W. D. 1963. "The Weakened Spring of Government: A Study in Nineteenth-Century American History." *American Historical Review* 68: 662–80.

Feagin, Joe R., Hernán Vera, Nikitah Imani. 1996. *The Agony of Education: Black Students at White Colleges and Universities*. New York and London: Routledge.

Ferretti, Fred. 1969. "Who's to Blame in the School Strike?" In *Confrontation at Ocean Hill–Brownsville*, pp. 283–313.

Foner, Philip S. 1976. *Organized Labor and the Black Worker: 1619–1973*. New York: International Publishers.

———, ed. 1995. *The Black Panthers Speak*, with a foreword by Claybourne Carson. New York: Da Capo Press.

Freire, Paulo. 1990. *Pedagogy of the Oppressed*. New York: Continuum.

Gates, Jr., Henry Louis. 1992. "Black Demagogues and Pseudo Scholars." *New York Times*, 20 July.

Gilroy, Paul. 1993. *The Black Atlantic: Modernity and Double Consciousness*. Cambridge, MA: Harvard University Press.

Goldberg, David Theo, ed. 1990. *Anatomy of Racism*. Minneapolis: University of Minnesota Press.

Goldbloom, Maurice. 1969. "The New York School Crisis." In *Confrontation at Ocean Hill–Brownsville*, pp. 247–82.

Gooding-Williams, Robert. 1993. *Reading Rodney King, Reading Urban Uprising*. New York: Routledge.

Gordon, Lewis R. 1995a. *Bad Faith and Antiblack Racism*. Atlantic Highlands, NJ: Humanities Press.

———. 1995b. *Fanon and the Crisis of European Man: An Essay on Philosophy and the Human Sciences*. New York and London: Routledge.

———. 1997a. *Her Majesty's Other Children: Sketches of Racism from a Neocolonial Age*. Lanham, N.Y., Boulder, CO, and Oxford: Rowman & Littlefield.

———. 1997b. "Introduction: Black Existential Philosophy." In *Existence in Black: An Anthology of Black Existential Philosophy*, ed. with an intro. by Lewis R. Gordon. New York and London: Routledge, pp. 1–10.

Gossett, Thomas F. 1965. *Race: The History of an Idea in America, 1900–1930*. Baton Rouge: Louisiana State University Press.

Gramsci, Antonio. 1971. *Selections from the "Prison Notebooks" of Antonio Gramsci*. Trans. and ed. Quintin Hoare and Geoffrey Nowell Smith. New York: International Publishers.

Goldbloom, Maurice J. 1969. "The New York School Crisis." In *Confrontation at Ocean Hill–Brownsville*, pp. 247–83.

Guinier, Lani. 1994. *Tyranny of the Majority*. New York: The Free Press.

Gutman, Herbert G. 1976. *The Black Family in Slavery and Freedom 1750–1925*. New York: Vintage.

Harnett, Patrick. 1969. "Why Teachers Strike: A Lesson for Liberals." In *Confrontation at Ocean Hill–Brownsville*, pp. 205–14.

Harrington, Michael. 1969. "The Freedom to Teach: Beyond the Panaceas." In *Confrontation at Ocean Hill–Brownsville*, pp. 129–36.

Hobsbawm, Eric J. 1987. *The Age of Empire, 1875–1914*. New York: Pantheon Books.

Horne, Gerald. 1994. "On the Criminalization of a Race." *Political Affairs* 73 (2) (February): 26–30.

Isaacs, Charles S. 1969. "A JHS 271 Teacher Tells It Like He Sees It." In *Confrontation at Ocean Hill–Brownsville*, pp. 192–205.

Jacoby, Russel. 1987. *The Last Intellectuals: American Culture in the Age of Academe*. New York: Basic Books.

James, Joy Ann. 1996. *Resisting State Violence in U.S. Culture*. Minneapolis: University of Minnesota Press.

————. 1997. *Transcending the Talented Tenth: Black Leadership in America*, with a Foreword by Lewis R. Gordon. New York: Routledge.

Jaynes, Gerald and Robin Williams, eds. 1989. *A Common Destiny: Blacks and American Society*. Washington, D.C.: National Academy Press.

Jefferson, Thomas. [1787]. *Notes on Virginia*. In *The Writings of Thomas Jefferson*, ed. Merrill D. Peterson. New York: The Library of America, 1984.

Kaestle, Carl F. 1983. *Pillars of the Republic: Common Schools and American Society (1780–1860)*. New York: Hill and Wang/ Farrar, Straus and Giroux, 1983.

Karp, Richard. 1969. "School Decentralization in New York." In *Confrontation at Ocean Hill–Brownsville*, pp. 63–76.

Kasinitz, Philip. 1992. *Caribbean New York: Black Immigrants and the Politics of Race*. Ithaca: Cornell University Press.

Kaufman, Jonathan. 1997. "Blacks and Jews: The Struggle in the Cities." In *Struggles in the Promised Land*, pp. 107–21.

Kemble, Eugenia. 1967. "New York Experiments in School Decentralization." *The United Teacher*, 20 December.

————. 1969. "Ocean Hill–Brownsville." In *Confrontation at Ocean Hill–Brownsville*, pp. 33–51.

Klein, Joe. 1995. "The End of Affirmative Action." *Newsweek*, 13 February, 36–37.

Landsman, Alter F. 1969. *Brownsville: The Birth, Development, and Passing of a Jewish Community in New York*. New York: Bloch Publishing Company.

Lawson, Bill E., ed. 1992. *The Underclass Question*. Philadelphia: Temple University Press.

Lerner, Michael and Cornel West. 1995. *Jews and Blacks: Let the Healing Begin*. New York: Grosset/Putnam.

Lester, Julius. 1988. *Love Song: Becoming a Jew*. New York: Arcade Publishing.

Lewis, Earl. 1997. "The Need to Remember: Three Phases in Black and Jewish Educational Relations." In *Struggles in the Promised Land*, pp. 231–55.

Lincoln, Abbey. 1961. "Straight Ahead." From *Straight Ahead*. New York: BMI and Columbia Records.

Madhubuti, Haki R. 1990. *Black Men: Obsolete, Single, Dangerous? The African American Family in Transition*. Chicago: Third World Press.

Madhubuti, Haki, John Henrik Clarke, Ishmael Reed, Delores Aldridge, and Tony Martin. 1993–1994. "Blacks, Jews, and

Henry Louis Gates, Jr.: A Response." *Black Books Bulletin: WordsWork* 16 (1)(2) (winter): 1–33.

Mansfield, E. D. 1851. *American Education, Its Principles and Elements*. New York: Barnes.

March, J. G. and J. P. Olsen. 1984. "The New Institutionalism: Organizational Factors in Political Life," *American Political Science Review* 78: 734–49.

Marx, Karl and Friedrich Engels. 1978. *The Marx-Engels Reader*. 2nd ed. Robert C. Tucker, ed. New York: W.W. Norton & Company.

Massey, Douglas S. and Nancy A. Dentin. 1993. *American Apartheid: Segregation and the Making of the Underclass*. Cambridge, MA: Harvard University Press.

McClellan, B. Edward and William J. Reese, eds. 1988. *The Social History of American Education*. Chicago: University of Illinois Press.

McCoy, Rhody. 1969. "The Year of the Dragon." In *Confrontation at Ocean Hill–Brownsville*, pp. 52–63.

McGary, Howard. 1999. *Race and Social Justice*. Oxford: Blackwell.

McIntyre, Charshee C. L. 1993. *Criminalizing a Race: Free Blacks During Slavery*. New York: Kayode.

Miller, Adam. 20 October, 1994. "Academia's Dirty Secret: Professors of Hate." *Rolling Stone*, pp. 106–14.

Moynihan, Daniel Patrick. 1965. *The Negro Family in America: A Case for National Action*. Washington, D.C.: Government Printing Office.

Morel, E. D. 1969. *The Black Man's Burden: African Colonial Labor on the Congo and Ubangi Rivers, 1880–1900*. Boulder, CO: Westview Press.

Naison, Mark. 1985. *Communists in Harlem During the Depression*. New York: Grove Press.

New York Civil Liberties Union Report. [1968]. "The Burden of the Blame: NYCLU Report on the Ocean Hill–Brownsville School Controversy," by Ira Glasser. In *Confrontation at Ocean Hill–Brownsville*, pp. 104–19.

Niemeyer Report. July 30, 1968. "An Evaluative Study of the Process of School Decentralization in New York City." The Final Report by the Advisory and Evaluation Committee on Decentralization to the Board of Education of the City of New York. Reprinted in *Confrontation at Ocean Hill–Brownsville*, pp. 101–103.

Omi, Michael and Howard Winant. 1994. *Racial Formations in the United States: From the 1960s to the 1990s*. 2nd ed. New York and London: Routledge.

Ornstein, Allan C., Daniel U. Levine, and Doxey A. Wilkerson. 1975. *Reforming Metropolitan Schools*. Pacific Palisades, CA: Goodyear Publishing Company, Inc.

Palmer, Colin. 1998. *Passageways: An Interpretive History of Black America*. Vol II: *1863–1965*. New York: Harcourt Brace College Publishers.

Perlman, Joel. 1988. *Ethnic Differences: Schooling and Social Structure among the Irish, Italians, Jews, and Blacks in an American City (1880–1935)*. Cambridge, UK: Cambridge University Press.

Pieterse, Jan Nederveen. 1992. *White on Black: Images of Africa and Blacks in Western Popular Culture*. New Haven and London: Yale University Press.

"Questions by the Teachers Who Are Teaching in the Ocean Hill–Brownsville Demonstration Project, Addressed to Mr. McCoy, the Unit Administrator, and Members of the Governing Board." December 1967. Special Collection of the Politics and Education Program at Teacher's College. New York City.

Ravitch, Diane. 1974. *The Great School Wars—New York City (1805–1973): A History of the Public Schools as Battlefield of Social Change*. New York: Basic Books.

Reports of the National Governors' Association, 1996.

Reports of the U.S. Department of Education. 1991.

Robinson, Cedric. 1983. *Black Marxism: The Making of the Black Radical Tradition*. London: Zed Press.

———. 1997. *Black Movements in America*. New York and London: Routledge.

Rossner, Robert. 1969. *The Year without an Autumn: Portrait of a School in Crisis*. New York: Richard W. Baron Publishing Company.

Samarin, William J. 1989. *The Black Man's Burden: African Colonial Labor on the Congo and Ubani Rivers, 1880–1900*. Boulder, CO: Westview Press.

Schultz, Stanley K. 1973. *The Culture Factory: Boston Public Schools (1789–1860)*. New York: Oxford University Press.

Shor, Ira and Paulo Freire. 1987. *A Pedagogy for Liberation: Dialogues on Transforming Education*. South Hadley, MA: Bergan and Garvey Publishers, Inc.

Silverstein, Ken and Alexander Cockburn. November 1, 1994. "Racism USA, 1994: For whom the Bell Curve Tolls." *Counter-Punch* 1, (19) 1–6.

Stein, Annie. 1970. "Containment and Control: A Look at the Record." In *Schools against Children: The Case for Community Control*, ed. Annette T. Rubenstein. New York: Monthly Review Press, pp. 21–49.

Stern, Sol. 1969. "'Scab' Teachers." In *Confrontation at Ocean Hill–Brownsville*, pp. 176–92.

Tyack, David. 1993. "School of Governance in the United States: Historical Puzzles and Anomalies." In *Decentralization and School Improvement*, pp. 1–32.

Tyack, David and Larry Cuban. 1995. *Tinkering Toward Utopia: A Century of Public School Reform*. Cambridge, MA: Harvard University Press.

Tyack, David and Elisabeth Hansot. 1982. *Managers of Virtue: Public School Leadership in America (1820–1980)*. New York: Basic Books Inc. Publishers.

Tyack, D., R. Lowe, and E. Hansot. 1984. *Public Schools in Hard Times: The Great Depression and Recent Years*. Cambridge, MA: Harvard University Press.

Walzer, Michael. 1997. "Blacks and Jews: A Personal Reflection." In *Struggles in the Promised Land*, pp. 401–9.

Weber, Max. 1946. *From Max Weber: Essays in Sociology*. Trans. with an intro. by H. H. Gerth and C. Wright Mills. New York: Oxford University Press.

West, Cornel. 1982. *Prophesy, Deliverance!: An Afro-American Revolutionary Christianity*. Philadelphia: Westminster Press.

———. 1993. *Race Matters*. Boston: Beacon Press.

Westley, Robert. 1996. "White Normativity and the Racial Rhetoric of Equal Protection." In *Existence in Black*. (See Gordon)

Wilson, William J. 1987. *The Truly Disadvantaged: The Inner City, the Underclass, and Public Policy*. Chicago: University of Chicago Press.

Wright, Richard. 1965. "I Tried to Be a Communist." In *The God That Failed*, ed. Richard Crossman. New York: Harper & Row.

Wylmore, Gayraud, ed. 1989. *African-American Religious Studies: An Interdisciplinary Anthology*. Durham and London: Duke University Press.

Zegeye, Abe, Leonard Harris, and Julia Maxted. 1991. *Exploitation and Exclusion: Race and Class in Contemporary U.S. Society*. London: Hans Zell Publishers.

Index

A. Philip Randolph Institute 104
Activist intellectuals 1
Ad Hoc Committee to Defend the
    Right to Teach 104
Adickes, Sandra 110–111
Administrative decentralization 5,
    40; definition of 8–15
Administrators 2–3, 8–9
African-American Teachers' Asso-
    ciation 54, 84
Allen, State Commissioner James
    Jr. 35, 108; the Allen Plan 35
Amirault, Chris xii
Antigua 117
Anti-Semitism 79, 108; anti-
    Semitic pamphlet 81; as distinct
    from anti-Zionism 81; as wed-
    ded to anti-liberalism 83
Arendt, Hannah 74–77, 123; on
    black students as violent 75
Asian Americans 78
Assimilation 16, 73
Augusto, Geri xiii
Autobiography of Malcolm X 27

Baldwin, James 70–73; on black–
    Jewish conflict 70–73; on color-
    blindness 73; on using the Holo-
    caust to excuse Jewish bigotry
    70; on Jewish failure to take
    racial asymmetry seriously 72;
    on Jewish similarity with blacks
    71–72; on Jews being recognized
    as contributors to the West 71;
    on Jews not being the source of
    the problem of anti-black racism

72; on Jews not being urged to be
    nonviolent 71; on white Jewish
    exploitation of the; black poor
    70; on white Jews becoming
    Christians 70; on why blacks
    can't wait 71
Bank Street School of Education
    44
Belgian Congo 71
Belgians 71; Black(s) 78; double
    standards held for black commu-
    nity 24; perceptions of efforts of
    black, Puerto Rican, and poor
    white community of Ocean
    Hill–Brownsville 1, 5, 8, 24, 53,
    70; Puerto Rican, and poor
    white community of Ocean
    Hill–Brownsville 1, 4; unity of
    black community 27
Blacks and self-government 18
Black critical intellectual tradition
    25
Black radical intellectual tradition
    27
Black political moderates 15
Black children 31
Black separatists 27; liberal black
    emancipatory projects 68; radical
    black emancipatory projects 68
Black poverty 97
Black nationalism 102
Blacks as engaged in politics of
    "gesture" 123
Blacks and white Jews 68; alliances
    of 94; antagonism 4, 101; litera-
    ture of changing relations
    between 68

Black Panther Party 3, 82
Black Power 4, 24–5; *Black Power* (by Stokely Carmichael and Charles Hamilton) 27; criticisms of nation of Israel 81; FBI targeting of as violent 30; multiracial platform of 26, 78; militancy 77; attacks on 79
Bloomfield, Jack 51, 97, 106
Board of Education, New York City 4, 10, 15, 31–35, 37, 39–40, 43, 46, 51–52, 57–58, 60, 62–63, 66, 76, 89, 95, 97, 100, 102, 107, 113–114; advisory committee of 56; decisions concerning new principals hired by governing board 55; duties and powers of 8, 57; as predominantly Jewish 81; rejection of Herman Ferguson 51
Board of Examiners 41
Board of Regents 62, 64, 119–120
Bogues, B. Anthony xiii
Bourgeois revolution, egalitarian claims of 25
Bronx High School of Science 118
Brooke, Senator Edward 82, 85
Brown, Deputy Superintendent 63
Brown, H. Rap (Jamil Andullah Al-Amin) 3, 84; as leader of SNCC 27
Brown v. Board of Education of Topeka Kansas (1954) 16, 96
Brownsville 37
Bryke, Anthony S. 13
Buhle, Paul and Robin Kelley 94–95; on black–Jewish conflict 68
Bundy, McGeorge 42
Bureaucracy 8; bureaucracies 14, 19–24, 118; bureaucratic ideals 21; as compared to premodern, feudalist forms 20;as a feature of capitalist market economies 20;

trained experts required for 22
Busing 33

Campbell, Leslie 83–90; critics of Campbell's pedagogy 87–88; multiracial community of supporters 88
Canarsie 34
Carmichael, Stokley (Kwame Ture) 24–25; on black leadership and community control 29; as co-author of *Black Power* 27; on economic exploitation and the failure of public schools 28–29; on economic inequality on the basis of race 29; as leader of SNCC 27; on white controlled school boards 27–28
Carson, Claybourne 68; on black–Jewish conflict 68
Carson, Sonny 83, 114
Centralization 12
Césaire, Aimé 25
Choice 10
City University of New York (CUNY) 117–122, 133 n.34; Baruch College 120; Brooklyn; College 43–44, 120; City College 117–118, 120, 122, 144 n.3; College of Staten Island 120; Hunter College 120; John Jay College 120; Lehman College 120, 144 n.2; Lehman Scholars Program 144 n. 2; Medgar Evers College 120; New York City Technical College 120; Queens College 43, 56, 60, 120; York College 120
City Wide Committee for Integrated Schools 31–35
Civil rights 3
Civil Rights Movement 24, 31, 42, 74, 88; as violent 73
Clark, Kenneth 96

Clark, Suzanne xii
Class 93–116; literature on 143
n.35; neoliberal theories of class
109
Clinton, President William 140
n.27
Cohen, Morris Raphael 144 n.3
Colored Power 79
Columbia University 53
COINTELPRO 30, 79
Comaroff, Jean xiii
Comaroff, John xiii
Comaroff, Josh xiii
Committee on Racial Equality
(CORE) 31
Communism 142 n.17
Communists 85, 142 n.17
Community Control 4–5, 7–19,
23, 62, 78, 94, 124; arguments
against 16, 18–19; defense of
16–18; definition of 15; propo-
nents of 16–17
Community Studies Program,
Queens College 60, 78
Conservatives 85
Cornell University 3
"Cultural literacy" 2

Decentralization 7–19, 23, 61, 78,
102; decentralizing legislation
62; romanticization of a decentralized past 63
Decolonization 29
Democracy, pursuit of 14–15;
democratic institutions 14;
democratic life 7, 124; the institutionalizing of democratic participation 13; participatory
democracy 75
Detroit, Michigan 18
Dietrich, Wendell xii
Disadvantaged Community's
Power 79
District 17 37, 95

Dominicans 78
Donovan, Superintendent Bernard
35, 43, 50–51, 63–64, 115
DosSantos, Karita xi
Douglass, Frederick vii; on power
88
Du Bois, W. E. B. 25
Dussel, Enrique 128 n.22

East Flatbush, NYC 37
East Harlem, NYC 32
Education News 84–86
Elmore, Richard. 11–14, 16; on
arguments for and against
decentralization 16; on decen-
traliztion 11–14; on misunderstandings of how schools work
14; on James Morone's
"democratic wish" 14
Equality before the law 20–21
Evans, Mark xiii
Evans, Robert xiii
Experimental district 40; disbanded 100; newly hired teacher
demographics 66
Experts 18

Fanon, Frantz 25, 29
Fantini, Mario 39
Federal Communications Com-
mission 91
Feldman, Paul 103
Feldman, Sandra 103
Ferguson, Herman 50–51, 54, 57, 83
Finkelstein, Norman 138 n.16
Ford Foundation 4, 39–40, 42–43,
48, 57, 95; grant to Ocean Hill-
Brownsville 46
Free Choice Transfer Plan 33
Freedom vii
Freedom Schools 66

Galamison, Reverend 31
Garel, Jack xiii

Garel, Joseph xiii
Garel, Lori xiii
Garel, Pat xiii
Garvey, Marcus 25–26
Gittell, Marilyn 127 n.1
Glasser, Ira 98–100; defense of local board 99
Goldbloom, Maurice J. 46
Goldstein, Harriet 48
Goldstein, Chancellor Matthew 119–122
Gordon, Jenny xiii
Gordon, Lewis R. xiv
Gordon, Mathieu xiii
Gordon, Sol 38
Gordon, Sula xiv
Gottsfeld, Harry 38
Gottsfeld-Gordon plan 38–40
Governing Board 4, 53–54, 57, 59, 61–63, 70, 78–79, 83, 98, 100; attempts to establish legitimacy 96; choice of multiracial group of principals 106; committee formed to design alternative standards for district supervisors 55; creation of paraprofessional training; programs 60; criticism of 1968 strikes 67; effort to fight charges of anti-Semitism 101; final proposal of 47; as a group on a self-aggrandizing quest for power 76; sensitivity to Jewish concerns 82; sponsored teacher training sessions 54; statement against anti-Semitism 80; teachers hired by 113–116; transfer of teachers 63; and UFT teachers 47–53
Great Depression 11
Greenpoint, NYC 32
Gross, Superintendent Calvin 33, 35; community disappointment with Gross's integration plan 33

Guinier, Lani, on group rights 140 n.27
Guernsey, Margo xii

Hamilton, Charles V. 27; on black leadership and community control 29; as co-author of *Black Power* 27; on economic exploitation and the failure of public schools 28–29; on economic inequality on the basis of race 29; on white controlled school boards 28
Harlem, NYC 30, 71, 119
Harlem Parents' Committee 31
Harnett, Patrick 94, 111–112
Harrington, Michael 82, 103
Harvard University's Afro-American Studies Department 3
Healey, Carol xii
Henry, Paget xiii, 117–119, 122
Henry, Roosevelt 117
Hermanns, Kris xii
High school diploma, necessity of 2
History, racist misrepresentations of 1
Holocaust 70, 92
Honest Ballot Association 44
Hoover, J. Edgar 30
Howard University 42

Imperialism 26
Institute for Advanced Study, Princeton, New Jersey 77
Institute for Elementary and Secondary Education xiii
Integration 16, 19, 63; black and Puerto Rican community proposals for 34; failed efforts 95; Intermediate School 55 (I.S. 55) 4, 38, 45; integrationist leaders 33; struggles in the North 26;

struggles in NYC public school system 30–31; white evasion of 35; white protests against 32–33; Steering Committee for I.S. 55 38, 43, 48–49

Intermediate School 201 (I.S. 201) 30, 35, 38; 1966 boycott of 35–36

Irish 67

Isaacs, Charles S. 67–68, 79, 113–115; description of teacher Leslie Campbell 83; on the governing board's sensitivity to Jewish concerns 82; recounting UFT disruption of his class 114–115

James, C. L. R. 25–26; on Black Power 25–26; critique of 26; on Stokely Carmichael 25; on U.S. race politics in the North and South 26

Jefferson, Thomas 25

Jewish Defense League (JDL) 91–92

Jews 65–92

Jewish liberalism 69–70, 92; as advocates of a particular form of liberalism that constructed governing board as illiberal 69; conflation of anti-Semitism and anti-Zionism 81; defense of white Jewish power 74; divergent position on Ocean Hill–Brownsville among Jews 69; obscuring black attempts to be heard 72; Jewish power as exclusive 79; reasons for rejecting Black Power 74

Junior High School 271 (J.H.S. 271) 271, 51, 89, 97, 106, 114

Junior High School 275 (J.H.S. 275) 275, 34

Johnson, Bil xii

Kaestle, Carl F. xi

Kahn, Tom 104

Kalodner, Howard 60

Karp, Richard 39, 54; on formation of Ocean Hill–Brownsville 38

Kaufman, Jonathan 96; on black–Jewish conflict 68; on charges of anti-Semitism as labor strategy 101

Kelley, Robin D. J. 94–95; on black–Jewish conflict 94

Kellock, Alan 113

Kemble, Eugenia, on Gottsfeld-Gordon plan 38

Keynes, John Maynard 109

King, Martin Luther Jr. 3, 34, 73, 84, 87; and march for sanitation workers 67; and the Poor People's March 67

Knies, Kenneth xii

Kretchmer, Jerry 105

Ku Klux Klan 123–124

Labor 94–116, 125

Latino communities 2, 94–95

Law, "public" and "private" 20–21; "law and order" 68

League for Industrial Democracy (LID) 103–104

Left, the 93–116; "Old" 93–94, 110

Lehrach, Karen xii

Lester, Julius xii, 89–92

Lewis, Earl 79; on black–Jewish conflicts 69

Liberalism 5, 94; anti-liberalism 83; color–blindness of 73; liberal capitalism 109; liberal dialogue 89; liberals 85, 103, 144 n.44; liberals as easy allies with conservative socialists 142–143 n.17

Lincoln, Abbey xiv

Linden Boulevard 34

Lindsay, Mayor John 40–42, 62, 66, 76, 85, 95
London Marxists 25

MacDonald, Dwight 82, 103
Malcolm X 3, 24, 29–31, 84, 87; autobiography of 27; on blacks being construed as violent 29; on black leaders 29; influence on Rhody McCoy 43; multiracial activism of 140 n.33
March, J. G. and J. P. Olsen, on institutions 11
Marchi, State Senator 62; the Marchi Bill 105
Marxism xii, 109
McCoy, Rhody. 47–48, 54, 59, 76, 97–100, 106–107, 114; appointment as project administrator 45–46, 49–50; biography of 42–43; on black-controlled schooling 82; as compared with black leaders from the Civil Rights Movement 42–43; December 1967 meeting with teachers and governing board 56; fighting for budget for staff 57; hopes for Ocean Hill–Brownsville 43, 61; nomination of Herman Ferguson 50–51; private meetings with Shanker 55; portrayed as militant and power-hungry 83; response to transfer requests 60; statement to black and Puerto Rican educators 61; statement on community control 61; unheated storefront office of 57;
McMains, Emily xii
Mersha, Sara xii
Millspaugh, Frank 91
Militancy, black militants 15, 66; the very different conceptions of labor and black militancy 137 n.5;

Minor, Dale 91
Modernity 22; "the underside of" 14
More Effective Schools (MES) program 38, 46, 48, 50

National Association for the Advancement of Colored People (NAACP) 31, 59, 96
National Governors' Association (1991) 10
National standards 10
Native Americans 2, 78
"Negro question" 26
Nepotism 18
New America 103
New Bridges 116
New York Civil Liberties Union Report. [1968]. 98
New York Teachers' Guild 53
New York University 42
Newton, Huey P. 3
Niemeyer, Dr. John H. 44
Niemeyer Committee 44, 50
Niemeyer Report [July 30th, 1968] 134 n.38
Nihilism 1, 125
Nystrom, Sandy 113

Ocean Hill 37–38
Ocean Hill–Brownsville 1–5, 15, 23–24, 29–54, 65, 78–79, 84, 87–88, 93–98, 108, 110, 124; community's criticisms of 1968 strike 67; community seeking control 7; community as supporters of "vigilantism" and black racism 64; evolution into a white–black power struggle 53–54; formation of 32–42; historians' views of 68; planning council 44; questions raised by 5; a scheme for greater community participation in 4

Oliver, Reverend Herbert 45, 50–51, 65, 82–83
O'Neill, John 106–107
Open Admissions at CUNY 117–119
Ornstein, Allan C., Daniel U. Levine, and Doxey A. Wilkerson. 8–10, 16; on community participation 9; on community control 16 critique of 9–10; on decentralization 8–9;

Padmore, George 25
Palestinians 81
Pan-Africanism 140 n.32
Parent-Teacher Associations (PTA) 9, 59
Parent-Teacher Committees 4
Parents Workshop for Equality 31
Perlstein, Tony xii
Police 63, 67, 107–108, 119
Policy talk 10
Policy on Decentralization 40–41
Powell, Adam Clayton 37
Power, vii, 2–3, 88; dispersion of 14
Powis, Father 37–40; and the 1967 voters' registration drive 43–44
Poynter, Ralph 83
Principals 8–9, 57; first Chinese and Puerto Rican principals hired in New York City 116
Professional educators 9, 15–18, 23, 64; accountability of 17, 49; "black" 18–19; failures of 15; racially biased competitive exams for 17, 129 n.29; rejections of community control 16
Professional standards, evocation of 16, 96
Progressive Era social critics 10
Public Education, and social mobility 2; "rationalization of" 19

Public Schools, 2, 124; citywide boycotts of in NYC 31; community participation in 4; depleted budgets of 17; everyday lives of 11; governance of 15; policies and efforts to reform 1
Puerto Rican(s) 1, 4, 5, 8, 30, 78;
Puerto Rican children 31, 52, 94
Puerto Rican community 95

Queens, NYC 32–33

Race, education and power 3;
Racial and ethnic favoritism 18
Racial injustice 5
Racial justice 1
Racism 17, 59, 78, 95
Ravitch, Diane, criticism of governing board proposal 46–47; criticism of the 1967 governing board election 44–45; on Gottsfeld-Gordon plan 38
Reports of the U.S. Department of Education (1991) 10
Restructuring 10–11
"Reverse discrimination" 16–17
Rockefeller, Governor 64
Rossner, Robert 93
Rousseau, Jean-Jacques 25
Royce Fellowship Committee xii
Russell, Stu 113
Rustin, Baynard 103–104

School boards 18; functions and powers of 15; reply to criticism of inexperience of new members 17
Schwartz, Gary 144 n.2
Segregation 16, 73; in New York City 30–42
Shachtman, Max 103
Shah, Seema xi
Shanker, Al 64–65, 101, 103, 105–107; on anti-Semitic poem

89, 91; biography of 53; domino theory of 106; private meetings with McCoy 56

Sizer, Theodore R. 13

Six hundred schools, 118–119, 122; as an index used in college admissions 118; definition of 42, 133 n.34;

Social and economic justice 1

Socialism 103

Socialists 142 n.17

Solomon, Dina xiii

Stern, Sol 103–104, 108, 110; on 1968 NYC teachers' strikes 66–67; criticism of UFT 97, 108; on white privilege creating white mediocrity 137 n.6

Student Nonviolent Coordinating Committee (SNCC) 3; rejection of non-black leadership of 27

Students 9

Student achievement 18

Suburbs 23; demographics of suburban versus urban schools 130 n.46; suburban parents 23;

Superintendent of schools 60

Teachers (*see also* UFT) unions 17; and "absenteeism" 58; class dynamics of 111–112; classism of 58–59; complaints of planning council's behavior 49-50; in conflict with Ocean Hill–Brownsville 68; criticisms of community control 58; dismissed as "racists" 112; drawn to profession by a belief in the need for social change 86; and the governing board 58; NYC teachers 93–94; racial conflicts among 58; role in the experimental district 48; split among 66; transfers of 63, 99; white teachers in favor of community

control, but not for Ocean Hill–Brownsville 58; who see students in communities like Ocean Hill–Brownsville as other people's children 2–3

Third World 26

Third World revolutionaries 1

Tucker, Eric xii

Tung, Irene xii

Tyack, David., 11, 14, 16; alluding to Adam Smith 11; on arguments for and against decentralization 16; on decentralization 10; on the "invisible hand of ideology" 11; on misunderstandings of how schools work 14; "Underclass" 109

Undergraduate Teacher Education Program, Brown University xii

United Federation of Teachers (UFT) 4–5, 37, 40, 48, 50, 58, 69, 76, 78–79, 89, 91, 92–116; 1967 Fall strike 52–53; in Albany 105; alliance with Civil Rights Movements 73; boycotts of Ocean Hill–Brownsville 64; class dynamics of 116; condemning black community as violent 73–75; demand for due process 66, 100; dissemination of anti-Semitic pamphlet 101; Fall 1968 NYC teachers' strikes 65–68; formation of 53; and the governing board 47–53; grievance procedures 63; hostility toward the governing board 55; joins with NYC Council of Supervisory Associations 55, 60, 62; newspaper support of 104; perception of strike as sign of opposition to community control 54; racist dimensions of strikes 67; strikes as **parents'** reason for keeping their children home from school 67; summer planning council 53; sued by Education News for misrepresentation of published transcript 84

United Negro Improvement Association (UNIA) 26

University of Illinois 53

Urban poor and immigrant children 2

Urban League 31, 59

U.S. citizens, distrust of government and centralization 10

Van Deburg, William L. on Black Power 26–27

Vietnam War 3

Violence and moral ambiguity 87; white reporters' efforts to connect Malcolm X to 29

Walker, Chas xii

Walzer, Michael 76–79, 122, 140 n.32; on Black Power as politics "of gesture" 77, 89; on "civil war" among Jews 116; on the need for building coalitions 77–78;

Washington, Booker T. 25

Washington, D.C. 42

Watts, LA 71

WBAI, NY 89–92

Weber, Max 5, 118; on bureaucracy 19–23; on "cultural capital" 22; on power 22; on "public" and "private" law 20–21; on the state 21;

"White flight" 19, 32

White liberals 15

"White Power" 5, 65–92

White power structure 27

Wilkins, Roy 50

Williamsburg, NYC 32

Williamson, Judy xiii

Wilson, Kate xiii

Wilson, Sage xii

Wilson, William J. 109

Wolf, Rabbi Arnold Jacob xiii, 144 n.44; on liberals 144 n.44

Working class 77

Woods, Tyrone 91

Yeshiva University 38

Yorkville, NYC 32

Young, Whitney 50

Young People's Socialist League 103